The Grammar Crammer

Books by Judi Kesselman-Turkel and Franklynn Peterson:

The Author's Handbook (Prentice-Hall, 1982)
The Grammar Crammer (Contemporary Books, 1982)
The Magazine Writer's Handbook (Prentice-Hall, 1982)
Note-Taking Made Easy (Contemporary Books, 1982)
Research Shortcuts (Contemporary Books, 1982)
Study Smarts (Contemporary Books, 1981)
Test-Taking Strategies (Contemporary Books, 1981)
The Vocabulary Builder (Contemporary Books, 1982)
Homeowner's Book of Lists (Contemporary Books, 1981)
How to Improve Damn Near Everything Around the House (Prentice-Hall, 1981)
I Can Use Tools (Elsevier/Nelson, 1981), illustrated by Tomas Gonzales
Good Writing (Franklin Watts, 1980)
Vans (Dandelion Press, 1979), illustrated by Paul Frame
Eat Anything Exercise Diet (William Morrow, 1979), with Dr. Frank Konishi
Handbook of Snowmobile Maintenance and Repair (Hawthorn, 1979)
The Do-It-Yourself Custom Van Book (Contemporary Books, 1977)

Books by Franklynn Peterson:

Children's Toys You Can Build Yourself (Prentice-Hall, 1978)
How to Fix Damn Near Anything (Prentice-Hall, 1977)
The Build-It-Yourself Furniture Catalog (Prentice-Hall, 1976)
Handbook of Lawn Mower Repair (Emerson, 1973; 2nd edition, Hawthorn, 1978)

Books by Judi R. Kesselman:

Stopping Out (M. Evans, 1976)

The Grammar Crammer

How to Write Perfect Sentences

Judi Kesselman-Turkel
and
Franklynn Peterson

CONTEMPORARY
BOOKS, INC.
CHICAGO

Library of Congress Cataloging in Publication Data

Kesselman-Turkel, Judi.
The grammar crammer.

Includes index.
Summary: Explains some of the more troublesome and confusing aspects of English grammar under the topics of nouns, pronouns, verbs, modifiers, sentences, conjunctions and prepositions, and punctuation. Includes practice quizzes.
1. English language—Grammar—1950- . 2. English language—Rhetoric. [1. English language—Grammar. 2. English language—Composition and exercises]
I. Peterson, Franklynn. II. Title.
PE1112.K43 1982 428.2 82-45413
ISBN 0-8092-5654-1 AACR2

Published by Contemporary Books, Inc.
180 North Michigan Avenue, Chicago, Illinois 60601
Manufactured in the United States of America
Library of Congress Catalog Card Number: 82-45413
International Standard Book Number: 0-8092-5654-1

Published simultaneously in Canada by
Beaverbooks, Ltd.
150 Lesmill Road
Don Mills, Ontario M3B 2T5
Canada

Because English grammar is in transition, relaxing outmoded rules to conform to reality, this book is not just for students in high school and college but also for adults who want a brief, sensible guidebook for business and personal writing.

CONTENTS

The Grammar Crammer

HOW TO USE THIS BOOK

CLUE 1: WHY WE HAVE TROUBLE WITH GRAMMAR

Whether or not we know a genitive from a gerund, we all know thousands of grammar rules. We had to learn them just to speak so that other people could understand us. Most of those rules came so easily we didn't even recognize them as rules. We learned instinctively when to say *I* and when to say *we.* We didn't have to be taught how to invert words in sentences to turn them into questions. We learned without all the Latin names in grammar textbooks, mostly by listening to other people speak.

But there are a few rules of grammar that trouble most of us. Some of the trouble comes because our speaking voices add accents and pauses that explain what we mean; sometimes the same words, written down, only confuse the reader. Some of the trouble comes because we learned many words by hearing them, not by seeing them, and what we thought we heard was not what was really being said. Some of the trouble comes because everyday life doesn't require many of the grammar constructions we need to use in writing. Some of the trouble comes because spoken language keeps changing, while written language lags behind. And some of the trouble comes because in some towns and neighborhoods the standard spoken language is a bit different from standard school English.

This book focuses on the rules in standard school English

that cause the most problems. Its *clues* show not only why you're called to task for using words and sentences that make perfect sense when you speak them, but how to change those constructions to satisfy even the most conservative grammarian. Its *catches* highlight especially tricky rules that trap the unwary.

We must warn you that this book isn't a total course in textbook grammar. It omits many technical grammatical problems. It avoids Latin terms unless there's no other way to explain what we mean. But we guarantee that, once you've read it, you'll know how to avoid most of the words and phrases that are considered ungrammatical.

CLUE 2: WHY GRAMMAR IS SO CONFUSING

Back in the eighteenth century, when the young sciences of physics, chemistry, and biology were dazzling the minds of men, a number of British writers tried to make the English language into a science. They called their science *grammar,* which in Latin means the study of the written word. They discovered some patterns in usage, and turned these patterns into rules. They not only divided sentences into subject and predicate, but classified words into parts of speech (nouns, verbs, conjunctions, and so forth) just as biologists classified plants and animals into groups. It wasn't long before American schools, too, were teaching English grammar.

But spoken English keeps changing. What was English in Chaucer's day reads like a foreign language now. Shakespeare's English, too, is very different from ours. Even some words and phrases that were correct in the eighteenth century are never used anymore today. To account for all these changes, instead of admitting that English isn't a science, grammarians soon separated the language into two parts: *colloquial* (that which is spoken) or *informal* English, and *script* (that which is written) or *formal* English. Until just a few years ago, all students were required to learn to write formal English and to know all the old rules the grammarians came up with, right or wrong. Nowadays there are three kinds of English: *colloquial,* which we speak among friends; *formal,* which we write when we want to impress; and *informal,* the language that was spoken in most places a decade or two ago, and which is now accepted for public speaking and for most writing.

Right now, the study of English grammar is undergoing a revolution. Experts like Noam Chomsky are rehabilitating our changing spoken language, making it respectable once more. They have thrown out many of the old rules. They tell us that sentences can't be separated easily into nameable parts because much of what we say is condensed from longer, more involved thought. They admit now that even parts of speech aren't easy to classify—something students have known since they struggled with the first grammar books.

In the English language, a word's part of speech actually depends on how it appears in the sentence:

NOUN: The *pen* is for pigs.
VERB: *Pen* the pigs in.
ADJECTIVE: A *penned* pig squeals.

That's why Lewis Carroll was able to write the poem *Jabberwocky,* which seems to make sense even though it's full of nonsense words:

'Twas brillig, and the slithy toves
Did gyre and gimble in the wabe . . .

Nobody has yet found a better way to organize an English grammar book, not even us. As we go along, however, we'll try to clear up some of the confusion caused by these artificial names for words.

1
NOUNS

It's important to be able to recognize nouns, because nearly every grammatically correct sentence must contain either a noun or its substitute, the pronoun.

CLUE 1: MOST NOUNS CAN FOLLOW *THE*

The word *noun* means name, and a noun names something. Some of the things it names are easy to remember:

Living things, whether real or imaginery, here on Earth or in outer space:

PERSON: John
girl
team

ANIMAL: dog
unicorn
menagerie

PLANT: yeast
vegetable
legume

Non-living things that take up space:

chair	dinnerware
star	farm
New York	atom

Many nouns are harder to recognize as *things:*

TITLES:	*Star Trek*
ATTRIBUTES:	softness
	ambition
	depth

Then there's a whole class of nouns that, for want of a better word, grammar books call *ideas:*

communism
information
quarrel
word

The best way to tell whether a word is a noun is to put *the* ahead of it. If you can use the phrase *the + (word)* to begin a sentence that makes sense, it's most likely a noun:

The crowd mills around the square.
The quarrel was stopped at last.
The depth of that water is scary.
The dancing went on and on.

Catch 1: Some Nouns Are Also Verbs

Notice that the word *dancing,* in the last example, becomes a verb if it changes place in the sentence:

The crowd is *dancing*.

That's true of most *-ing* words. Many grammars call them *verbals;* some grammars also call them *gerunds.*

Verbals don't change spelling at all when they become nouns:

VERB: Folks have been crowding into me.
NOUN: Crowding isn't permitted.

But many verbs (and other words) become nouns by adding *-tion, -ity, -ism, -ment, -ness,* and other endings:

absorb	absorption
embezzle	embezzlement

Catch 2: Some Nouns Are Groups of Words

Even more confusing than the nouns that look just like verbs are the *compound nouns* and *noun phrases.* They come in many shapes and sizes.

Compound nouns (see also page 14) are nouns or other parts of speech put together to mean something new. Eventually most become one word:

breakthrough
dropout
coffeepot

But they always start off as two words:

candy striper
coffee table

Some go through an intermediate hyphenated phase:

higher-up
father-in-law

The only way to be sure of the spelling of these words is to use a dictionary.

Some group nouns are destined never to combine into one word:

> the King of England
> The Mill on the Floss
>
> *The doctor and the dentist* share an office.

Noun phrases can't be found by using *the* +. Some can be located because they're the only subject in the sentence:

> *Whoever comes* is welcome.
> *Choosing a major* isn't easy.
> *After dinner* is too late to go.

But some are objects, not subjects:

> The boss docks *anyone late.*

To double-check a suspected noun phrase, substitute a pronoun. The sentence should still make sense:

> *He* is welcome.
> *It* isn't easy.
> *It* is too late to go.
> The boss docks *him.*

A special group noun is the *verbal infinitive, to + (verb):*

> *To study* isn't always fun.

Here's a verbal-infinitive noun phrase:

> *To do the work* required extra care.

Notice that when verbal infinitives are used as verbs, not nouns, they always come after auxiliary verbs. (For auxiliary verbs, see page 42.)

NOUN: It isn't always fun *to study.*
VERB: I *am going to study* tomorrow.

CLUE 2: MOST NOUNS ADD *S* TO SHOW PLURAL

The vast majority of nouns change meaning from *one* to *many* by adding *-s:*

boy	boys

If the noun already ends in -s, -ss, -ch, -sh, or -x, we add *-es:*

grass	grasses
lens	lenses
box	boxes
witch	witches

If the noun ends in *-lf* or *-fe,* we change the ending to *-ve* and add *-s:*

werewolf	werewolves
wife	wives

If the noun ends in *-y,* we change it to *-i* and add *-es:*

city	cities

If the noun ends in *-o* there isn't any set rule because the language is changing:

potato	potatoes

pro	pros
ghetto	ghettos or ghettoes

Your best bet here is to consult a dictionary and choose the first spelling (the preferred one) if two are shown.

Catch 3: Some Nouns Form Irregular Plurals

A few very old English words form plurals with *-en:*

child	children
ox	oxen
man	men
woman	women

Words that come from Latin hang onto their Latin plurals for a long time:

alumnus	alumni
dictum	dicta or dictums

BUT:

deus ex machina	deus ex machinas

Catch 4: Some Singular Nouns Have Plural Meanings

Several kinds of nouns conspire to confuse us. One is the *collective noun,* the word that stands for a group of whatevers. It uses singular to mean one group, plural to mean many groups:

a *flock* of geese	ten *flocks* of geese
a *bevy* of girls	six *bevies* of girls
a *family* of six	six *families*

Other nouns are almost always used in the singular, though they can mean more than one. Some grammars call them *uncountables:*

lots of *money*
several pages of *information*
a great deal of *friction*

Some nouns can be used in the singular to show an abstract idea, and in the plural to make the idea more specific or more tangible:

the green grass	many kinds of grasses
Tell me your trouble.	Tell me your troubles.

Note that the singular form doesn't show whether one or several grasses or troubles are being discussed, but the plural form can *only* mean more than one.

For some of these words that don't form simple plurals, a good dictionary can help you figure out correct usage. But in many cases, the dictionary offers no guidance. The best advice we can give is to notice the way educated people use singular and plural, and then listen to your inner ear when you write.

CLUE 3: POSSESSIVES CAN SHOW MORE THAN POSSESSION

Showing close relationships between nouns often causes confusion. Some of it comes because we've been taught young to call words like *boy's* and *children's* "possessives." With living things the relationship is usually actual ownership:

the boy's gun

But the possessive can also show an attribute or aspect:

the book's pages
the snow's whiteness
the tabletop's dust

Or it can be just a shorthand, turned-around way of saying *of:*

freedom's boundaries = the boundaries of freedom
a stone's throw = a throw of a stone

Possessive is a poor English translation of the Latin word *genitive,* which was a mistranslation by Latin grammarians of a Greek word that means *generic:* belonging to a large group. It's best to forget both *possessive* and *genitive* outside grammar class, and think of these simply as nouns that take *'* or *'s.*

Catch 5: Apostrophes Are Tricky

Many grammar books give rule after rule about forming possessives. The best rule is to write the singular or plural word you mean (using the guidelines we've given) and then to listen to the way you speak the phrase. If you add an extra *z* sound in speaking, show that in writing with *'s:*

John's book
the class's teacher
Oz's wizard
the lens's cap
Jack's forgetting his books made me angry.

If you don't add a *z* sound, just add an apostrophe:

snakes' venom
several quarters' worth

Group nouns take the *'* or *'s* on the last word:

the King of England's throne
The Mill on the Floss's plot
somebody else's chair

But for most long groups, it's easier—and usually clearer—to turn the sentence around:

NOT: This is whoever took its glass.
BUT: This glass belongs to whoever (or: *whomever*) took it.

NOT: the boy on the horse's right ear
BUT: the right ear of the boy on the horse

To show joint ownership by a group, add *'* or *'s* at the end:

the doctor and dentist's office	=	an office shared by one doctor and one dentist
the doctors and dentists' offices	=	several offices shared by several doctors and several dentists

Many teachers prefer that you punctuate each noun in the possessing group:

the doctors' and dentists' offices
the doctor's and dentist's offices
the doctors' and dentist's office

It's purely an arbitrary decision.

Catch 6: Compound Nouns Often Replace Possessives

For many close relationships, the English language offers an alternative to the possessive. It's the *compound noun* (see also page 7):

the chair's leg	the chair leg
the dance's step	the dance step

In fact, some of these compound nouns have been around so long, they're written today as one word:

the sun's light	the sunlight
the snake's pit	the snakepit
the mole's hill	the molehill

Some are in transition, and are still hyphenated:

the knife's edge	the knife-edge

When do you choose the compound noun, and when the possessive? In general, when you want the reader to come away with a stronger picture of the thing being "possessed" than of the possessor, choose the compound noun. If you want the possessor to assume equal or greater importance, choose the possessive:

The sunlight was blinding.	=	A particular light was blinding.
The sun's light was blinding.	=	The light that was blinding came from the sun.
I stepped on a molehill.	=	I stepped on a particular hill.
I stepped on a mole's hill.	=	The hill I stepped on was made by a mole.

CHECKUP QUIZ

1. For each of the words listed below, in the first column (*noun?*) mark (A) if it's always a noun, (S) if it's sometimes a noun, or (N) if it's never a noun. If it is always or sometimes a noun, write the singular possessive form in the second column and the plural possessive form in the third column.

	noun?	*sing. poss.*	*pl. poss.*
roar			
ligament			
life raft			
size			
equally			
droopy			
lift-off			
equation			
brass			
Jones			
lady			
who			
craze			
to			
lens			
to dream			
so			
equate			
Staten Island			
very			
dinnerware			
pity			
blessing			
to blossom			
communism			
dancing			
elf			
ghetto			
anybody else			

2. Give the alternate form for the following possessive relationships. (You may consult a dictionary.)

piano's player
nail's brush
nail's file
bird's seed
goose's down
moon's beam
comet's tail
guest's towel
war's victims
community's citizens
communism's philosophy

3. Underline every noun in the following paragraph.

Don Roux, who's in the business of promoting sweepstakes, knows how skeptical some people can be about them. So he delights in telling how he recently demonstrated sweepstakes' appeal to 35 professors of marketing during a seminar at Wayne State University. When he asked how many were not motivated by games of chance, six professors stuck up their hands. After an hour's lecture, Roux, 48, announced that he had taped his business card to the bottom of one chair and would send a free stereo to the person who found it. "Boy, you should have seen those six skeptics turning over chairs along with everybody else," he says.*

---

* Excerpted from "Catching Customers with Sweepstakes" by Peterson and Kesselman-Turkel, *Fortune,* February 8, 1982.

2
PRONOUNS

Pronouns cause a lot more confusion in writing than nouns, partly because grammarians made up some rules that aren't used in speech—and weren't in writing either until the rules were invented. But most errors creep in because some pronouns have several forms and the pronoun's place in the sentence determines the correct form.

CLUE 1: PRONOUNS COME IN SMALL GROUPS

If it's any comfort, English pronouns used to be far more complicated than they are now:

I am	*We* are
Thou art	*You* are
He / *She* / *It* } is	*They* are

When the singular of *you* was *thou,* the singular of *to you* was *to thee, your home* was *thy home,* and *yours* was *thine.* When the *thee* forms died out, somewhere around the seventeenth century, it made life a lot easier for students. Some of the other forms are fading fast from spoken American English, but in standard school English they're alive and kicking. If any of the pronouns in the table on the following page are unfamiliar to you, memorize them.

The first group is called *definite* pronouns, because they refer to one or more definite persons or things. Among them are the *personal pronouns,* which change form depending on how they're used.

Notice that all forms of *you* are the same in singular and plural except the reflexive, *yourself* changing to *yourselves* when it's more than one. We've also italicized the other irregularities that cause trouble.

There are two other groups of definite pronouns. The *demonstrative* pronouns show or point to a noun: *this, that, these, those.* (*Them* is not a demonstrative pronoun. In standard English it's incorrect to say or write *Look at them shoes.*) The *relative* pronouns have two jobs at once: they not only stand in for nouns, but at the same time they introduce clauses. They are:

> who, whoever, whom, whomever, whose (but not whosever; it's not a word), which, whichever, what, whatever, that

For more on relative pronouns, see page 25.

There's also a group of words that are sometimes pronouns, sometimes other parts of speech. When used as pronouns, they're called *indefinite pronouns* because they don't refer to anyone or anything in particular:

> one, anyone, someone, no one, everyone, either one, neither one
> anybody, somebody, nobody, everybody
> either, neither
> each, each one, each other

Personal Pronouns

	subjective	objective	possessive		reflexive
	(subject of sentence or clause)	*(object of verb)*	*with noun*	*without noun*	*(used for object when it's the same person or thing as the subject)*
singular	I	me	my	mine	myself
	you	you	your	yours	yourself
	he, she, it	him, her, it	hi*s*, her, it*s*	his, hers, its	*him*self, herself, itself
plural	we	us	our	ours	our*selves*
	you	you	your	yours	your*selves*
	they	them	their	theirs	*themselves*
interrogative (questioning)	who	(*whom*)	who*se*	whose	himself, herself, itself; *themselves*

Each used as a pronoun:

Each of us is going.	=	Jane, Bob, and I are going.

Each used as an adjective:

Eat some citrus each day.	=	Eat some one day and some another day. (*Each* doesn't substitute for *day* or *citrus*.)

The indefinite pronouns rarely cause trouble, even when you can't decide on the correct grammatical name.

Catch 1: Is It *I* or *me*?

In spoken language, people say "It's me" or "It is me" and the meaning is clear as rain:

List A

It's me.	It's us.
It's you.	It's you.
It's him.	It's them.
It's her.	

This use of the *objective case* after forms of the verb *be* is proof that English keeps changing despite the stranglehold of the grammarians. They'd love us all to use the *subjective case* after *be:*

List B

It is I.	It is we.
It is you.	It is you.
It is he.	It is they.
It is she.	

The evolution of *it is me* is worth tracing. In Old English, the order of our words was more like German than Modern English. Folks used to say *Ic hit eom,* which translates as *I it am.* In Middle English the *h* dropped off the word *it* and folks turned the phrase around to both *It I am* and the more popular *It am I.* Since *it* suddenly seemed like the subject of the sentence, *am* slowly became *is.* By the time Modern English was born, everyone said *It is I.* However, because *me,* not *I,* usually follows a verb, by the nineteenth century even Jane Austen was writing *It is me.*

Nonetheless, grammarians of the eighteenth century had been attacking this evolutionary change. Clinging to the belief that the old way of speaking was always more correct than the new way, they devised a complicated special rule about verbs that show existence. The rule persists in grammars to this day.

Our suggestion is that you learn the old forms (list B) so that you can use them whenever an eighteenth-century holdover is marking your papers for grammar. But in most writing, as in most speaking, you're perfectly correct if you use list A, the forms that come naturally.

Catch 2: *Whom* Isn't Dead Yet

Once upon a time the pronoun *who* had as many forms as all the other pronouns. They slowly disappeared and we were left with:

who whom whose

Then, as *thou* was being dropped entirely, *whom* came into disuse:

Middle English: Whom seekest thou?
Modern English: Who are you looking for?

The word *whomever* has fallen into much the same disuse. In fact, both words are so little used nowadays, we've caught some stilted writers trying to appear grand by using whom and whomever without knowing where these old words go.

To avoid looking silly yourself, we suggest you avoid these semi-archaic words unless your audience uses them regularly. If you must use them, keep in mind that they fit in as the *object* of a verb or preposition. (*Who* and *whoever* are used as subjects.)

WITH VERB: Whom are you *escorting?* (As the object of a verb, *whom* is used mostly in questions.)
WITH PREPOSITION: I know *for* whom the bell tolls.

To test whether you need *who* or *whom,* substitute *he* and *him* or *they* and *them* and decide which form is closer to your meaning:

CORRECT: (Whom) are you escorting *him?*
CORRECT: I know for (whom) *him* the bell tolls.
WRONG: Do you know whom is going?
TO CORRECT: Do you know (if) *he* is going?
WRONG: We hire persons whom we think work well.
TO CORRECT: We hire persons (when) we think *they* work well.
WRONG: There's no doubt as to whom should be elected.
TO CORRECT: There's no doubt, *he* should be elected.

To test whether you need *whoever* or *whomever,* insert *the person* and use the above test to choose between *who* and *whom:*

CORRECT: Take this to whomever we gave the ball.
PROOF: Take this to *the person* to whom we gave the ball.

Take this to the person; to *him* we gave the ball.

WRONG: Give this to whomever asks first.

PROOF: Give this to *the person who* asks first.
Give this to *the person;* he asks first.

CORRECTION: Give this to whoever asks first.

CLUE 2: HOW TO TELL A POSSESSIVE FROM A CONTRACTION

As we saw in Chapter 1, all nouns show possession with apostrophes. So do all the indefinite pronouns. But *definite pronouns never use apostrophes.* Look again at the chart (on page 19) to see how they form possessives.

Whenever a personal pronoun includes an apostrophe, it's always to show that two words have been put together and there's a letter missing. In the previous sentence, *it's* is short for *it is* and *there's* is short for *there is.* These words are called *contractions:* they contract a pronoun and a verb into one word and the verb is always *is* if the ending is *'s.* (For more on contractions, see p. 44.)

The its/it's confusion is so rampant, even ads often contain the wrong spelling. So in this case, don't copy what you read. Instead, stick to the simple rule that *its* never takes an apostrophe unless it means *it is.* (In your enthusiasm over getting *its* right, don't drop the apostrophe from *one's* in expressions like *a room of one's own. One* is not a personal pronoun but an indefinite one.)

Let's clear up two similar confusions while we're at it. *Theirs* is the pronoun, *there's* the contraction for *there is. Whose* is the pronoun, *who's* the contraction for *who is.*

CLUE 3: SOME PRONOUNS DEFY LOGIC

When the English language dropped its *thees* and *thous*

and turned *you* into singular as well as plural, it was a simple step for people to start making new plurals for *you.* In some places folks said *you-all,* in others *you-uns,* and still elsewhere *youse* became entrenched. One or all of these plurals might have eventually become correct if grammarians hadn't locked us into *you.* But we are locked in, so make sure you avoid any of the variant forms—whether speaking or writing—once you leave the safety of your neighborhood.

Another place where colloquial logic has lost out to grammatical rule is in adding *self* (singular) and *selves* (plural) to pronouns. Most of the pronouns form this *reflexive case* using the with-noun possessive root (the third column in our chart on page 19). But the *he* and *they* forms add it to the *objective.* People persist in trying to make sense out of chaos. That's why *hisself* and *theirselves* are heard all around us. But take warning: they're considered substandard English. The correct forms are:

himself themselves

The third place where you have to abandon logic when using pronouns is when you're pointing to a specific object. *These, those, this,* and *that* don't change form, but *them* changes to *those* when it's used like an adjective with the noun it refers to:

Hand me *that.* Hand me *that* book.
Hand me *these.* Hand me *these* books.
Hand me *those.* Hand me *those* books.

BUT:

Hand me *them.* Hand me *those* books.

Catch 3: The *which/that* Dilemma

The relative pronoun *which* is to *who* what *it* is to *he* and *she. Who* is used in statements and questions when describing people, and *which* is used when referring to animals and things. Few native English speakers have trouble differentiating between *who* and *which.* But another word, *that,* can refer to persons, animals, or things—and that causes all kinds of confusion to careful writers.

The problem came about because, when English was new, *that* was pretty much the only *relative pronoun* (a pronoun that relates the subject before it to the action coming after it):

> The boy that stole the book was crying.
> (subject: The boy; action: stole)

The only time *which* replaced *that* was in a question:

> Which stole the book? (Modern: Which one stole the book?)

Then people began using *which* and *that* interchangeably in declarative sentences and the grammarians, shuddering at this confusion, stepped in with some rules. Several contradictory rules still prevail, but the one in most grammar books is as follows:

Use *that* (or *who*) to introduce a limiting or defining clause, and *which* (or *who*) to introduce a clause that isn't needed to define the subject.

> DEFINING: The river that flows through New York is muddy.
> NONDEFINING: The river, which flows through New York, is muddy.

Since most grammar teachers understand the rule, they like to point out its infractions on students' papers. Here's how to get it right: Use *which* (or *who*) if the phrase it introduces belongs between commas as a parenthetical statement; otherwise, use *that.*

Until recently it was considered correct to interchange *that* and *who:*

> The boy who went home left his lunch behind.
> The boy that went home left his lunch behind.

Although spoken English still interchanges them, some overzealous grammar instructors are beginning to mark *that* wrong when it refers to persons. (For further discussion, see page 84.)

Catch 4: The *whose* Confusion

While *who,* as we've just shown, refers just to people, *whose* is used to refer to anything—persons, things, even ideas. It is the possessive form of *who,* of *which,* and of *that:*

> The river whose flow is through New York is muddy.
> The river, whose flow is through New York, is muddy.
> INCORRECT: It's an idea what's time has come.

Make sure that you spell this *whose* correctly. (*Who's* is the contraction for *who is.*)

CLUE 4: HOW TO USE THE PRONOUN *ONE*

The pronoun *one* comes from an altogether different word from the number *one,* a noun, even though today they're spelled and pronounced alike. The pronoun *one* is most commonly used as a shorthand for "he or she, it doesn't matter who" when it's the subject of the sentence. Once one uses one as the subject, one ought to continue its use through the sentence, but it generally ends up sounding so forced, writers change to *himself* or *herself* halfway through.

> One has to look out for his own neck.
> One can't take herself seriously all the time.

In England, *one* is used a great deal more than in the United States. Here, people rarely speak the word. Even in written English, Americans find ways to get around the construction:

> A person has to look out for his own neck.
> People can't take themselves seriously all the time.

Now that the women's rights movement has made many of us sensitive to the inadequacies of English pronouns, we may see a revival of the word *one* to get us out of the he/she dilemma. If so, we'll have to learn how to spell the possessive form. To distinguish from the plural noun *ones,* which means *persons,* the pronoun *one's* takes the apostrophe. It is the *only* personal pronoun that takes the apostrophe to form its possessive:

> PRONOUN: One is not to scribble in *one's* books.
> NOUN: They are the *ones* I meant.

Notice that the noun, too, has a possessive form:

> PLURAL NOUN POSSESSIVE: Take care of the little *ones'* clothing.

CLUE 5: THE VERBS THAT FOLLOW INDEFINITE PRONOUNS

It's clear that *one* is singular and takes a singular verb.

One is, never *one are.* However, there's a small group of indefinite pronouns that have *one* in them, or imply the word *one,* that give us all verb trouble:

> either, either one
> each, each one
> any, anyone, anybody
> everyone, everybody
> none, no one, nobody
> neither, neither one

In speaking, most of us always correctly use the singular verb with *anyone* and *anybody:*

> *Anyone* around my base *is* it.
> If *anybody wants* this, he can have it.

But with the rest of the list, we often shift to the plural if there's an intervening modifying phrase:

> *Everyone is* late for breakfast today.
> *Everyone of us are* late for breakfast today.
> *Neither horse has* been shod yet.
> *Neither of the horses have* been shod yet.

Some grammars try to suggest a distinction between the negative words and the positive ones. They point out that all the positive words mean *one person* (even *everybody* and *everyone,* which were originally *every body* and *every one*), and should therefore take singular verbs to be grammatically correct. But since the negative verbs refer to the absence of people, only *neither one* should always take the singular; the rest, they say, can take whatever sounds best to you.

Such a rule seems completely illogical. We suggest that you *say* whatever you like, whatever sounds most comfortable. When it comes to writing, if you think someone's going to be evaluating your grammar, stick to the singular verb after each one of these words.

CHECKUP QUIZ

1. In the following sentences, underline all the pronouns. If a pronoun is gramatically incorrect, correct it.

a. The pianist, who studied with Rubenstein, started his career with a recital.
b. He's making hisself sick.
c. Nobody does it better.
d. Hand me one of them books.
e. Each of these companies had its books audited.
f. One needs to see her dentist twice a year.
g. One has to live with themself.
h. Nearly everybody gets married and unmarried and married again but they're all married to someone most of the time.
i. The women kept it between theirselves.
j. Every man and woman shows their stuff some time in life.
k. The choir is writing their own songs.
l. The members don't agree on their methods but they do agree on how to implement it.

2. Fill in the most proper word, spelled correctly.

a. The dog licked ______ chops. (his, its, it's)
b. You'll get ______, he'll get ______, and they'll get ______. (yourn, your's, yours; hisn, his', his; theres, there's, theirs)
c. ______ books are those on the table? (Who's, Whos, Whose)
d. Nobody takes ______ seriously any more. (himself, hisself, itself)
e. ______ the boy ______ house we spent the night at. (Theirs, There's, Theres; whose, whos, who's)

f. It is ______ ______ you spoke to on the phone. (I, me; who, whom)
g. Give the ticket to ______ rings the bell. (whoever, whomever)
h. ______ are you taking to the dance? (Who, Whom)
i. One can't turn on the radio without having music blare out at ______. (him, her, it, one, him or her.)
j. ______ own parents ______ the last to know. (Ones, One's, Ones'; is, are)
k. Neither rain nor snow nor sleet ______ the mail carrier. (stop, stops)
l. Everybody ______ the dance. (do, does)
m. Each ______ ______ own work. (do, does; his, their, they're)
n. ______ was a nervewracking presence. (They'res, Theirs, Their's, Theirs')
o. ______ ______ who ______ taking the last train out of here. (It's, Its; I, me; am, is)
p. ______ is a better television set than mine. (They'res, Theirs, They're, Their)
q. Either you or ______ ______ right, but not the two of ______. (I, me; am, are, is; we, us)

3
VERBS

Most people have little trouble identifying verbs by the time they get to high school. If a word makes sense with *to* in front of it, it's probably a verb—though many verbs, like nouns and pronouns, sometimes shift into other parts of speech.

In Spanish, German, Latin, and many other languages, lots of words change their endings to show such things as *person* (whether one or many males, females, or neuters), *degree of comparison,* and *tense.* In English, aside from a few nouns (*person:* waiter, waitress) and modifiers (*degree of comparison:* fast, faster, fastest), the only other words that change are the verbs, and most of them have only two big changes, for *third person singular* and *past tense.*

Today nearly every English verb forms its third person singular (the *he, she, it* form) by adding *-s,* while all the other persons keep the unchanged form of the verb. Four exceptions to this rule are *go* and *do,* which add *-es; have,* which drops the *ve* in third person singular (*ha(ve)s);* and *be,* which has many distinct forms.

Today, too, most of our English verbs change tense in the same exact way: by adding *-ed* for simple past tense and for past participle (the ending used with *have*).

I work   I worked   I have worked

Few people have trouble with these verbs. However, when English began, it was much more like the other languages. Almost every verb changed significantly to show tense, and there were about a half dozen distinct patterns of change. Of these verbs, now among the oldest verbs in English, about 150 survived pretty much intact even when all the new verbs that were being formed conformed to the simplest and most-used endings.

CLUE 1: MEMORIZE TRICKY IRREGULAR VERBS

As we've pointed out, our spoken language keeps changing all the time, and one way is by leveling out the irregularities. Since so many irregularities occur in verb tense forms, it's not surprising that many verbs are in transition. For some verbs, two accepted forms (according to *Webster's New Collegiate Dictionary,* 8th edition) exist side by side. For some, one spoken alternate is still considered unacceptable by grammarians. For some, the newer version has almost driven out the old one.

We've listed the accepted forms of all the irregular verbs, starring (*) the ones that cause students most writing trouble. We suggest that you test your knowledge of them all, and then memorize those you're unsure of just as if you were learning a foreign language. To help you memorize, we've arranged the verbs into groups. If a verb form that's used in your neighborhood isn't on the list (for instance, *drug* for the past tense of *drag*), it's considered illiterate by most grammarians; avoid it anywhere you wouldn't go in your pajamas.

VERBS THAT DON'T CHANGE

The simple forms are used for both present and past

events. (These verbs are pushing hard toward regularization, and many now have accepted regular alternates, as shown.)

1. Verbs without alternates

*cast	*hit	*set	*split
*cost	hurt	*shed	*spread
cut	put	*slit	*thrust

2. Verbs with alternates

simple	*past*	*past participle*
bet	bet, betted	bet, betted
bid†	bid, bade	bid, bidden, bade
burst	burst, bursted	burst, bursted
bust††	bust, busted	bust, busted
let	let, letted†††	let, letted†††
quit	quit, quitted	quit, quitted
rid	rid, ridded	rid, ridded
wed	wed, wedded	wed, wedded
wet	wet, wetted	wet, wetted

† *bade* and *bidden* are old forms, rarely used any more.

†† Many grammarians consider *bust* illiterate. Avoid it in formal writing.

††† *letted* is used only when there is a direct object: *The nurse letted blood.*

VERBS WITH JUST ONE PAST FORM

1. *Final consonant changes to* t. (Notice that next-to-final consonant is *l* or *n*.)

simple	*past*
bend	bent
build	built

simple	*past*
dwell	dwelt, dwelled
*lend	lent
*rend	rent
send	sent
spend	spent

2. *Changes to* ght. (Notice which two are spelled with *au*.)

simple	*past*
*bring	brought
*buy	bought
*catch	caught
*fight	fought
*seek	sought
*teach	taught
*think	thought

3. *Vowel* i *(long* i*) changes to* ou.

simple	*past*
*bind	bound
find	found
*grind	ground
wind	wound, winded

4. *Vowel* ee *changes to* e.

simple	*past*
*bleed	bled
*breed	bred
*creep	crept
*feed	fed
*feel	felt
flee	fled
keep	kept
kneel	knelt

simple	*past*
meet	met
*sleep	slept
*sweep	swept
*weep	wept

5. *Vowel* ea *stays* ea *with different pronunciation.*

simple	*past*
deal	dealt
dream	dreamt, dreamed
mean	meant
read	read

6. *Vowel* ea *changes to* e.

simple	*past*
*lead	led
leave	left
plead	pleaded, pled†

† *Pled* should be avoided in formal writing.

7. *Vowel* i *changes to* u. (Don't confuse these with verbs with two past forms going from *i* to *a* to *u*.)

simple	*past*
*cling	clung
*dig	dug
*fling	flung
sling	slung
slink	slunk, slinked
*spin	spun
*stick	stuck
*sting	stung
string	strung
*swing	swung
*wring	wrung

8. *Other vowel and consonant changes.*

simple	*past*
come	came
dive	dove, dived
*hang	hung, hanged†
have	had
hear	heard
hold	held
*lay	laid
light	lit, lighted
*lose	lost
make	made
pay	paid, payed††
run	ran
say	said
sell	sold
shine	shone, shined†††
*shoe	shod
shoot	shot
*sit	sat
*slide	slid
stand	stood
strike	struck
*tell	told
win	won

† *Hanged* is the past tense only when one means *put to death by hanging.*

†† *Payed* is the past tense when one means *allowed to run out: He payed out the rope.*

††† *Shined* is the past tense when one means *polished.*

VERBS WITH TWO PAST FORMS.

The verbs listed here are the only ones with special past participle forms. Notice that many are changing.

1. *Vowel changes from* i *to* a *to* u. (Don't confuse these with previous list of verbs changing *i* to *u*.)

simple	*past*	*participle*
*begin	began	begun
drink	drank	drunk, drank
*ring	rang†	rung†
shrink	shrank, shrunk	shrunk, shrunken
sing	sang, sung	sung
sink	sank, sunk	sunk
spring	sprang, sprung	sprung
stink	stank, stunk	stunk
*swim	swam	swum

† *Ringed* is both past and past participle when one means *formed a ring around.*

2. *Changes only in past.*

simple	*past*	*participle*
*come	came	come
*run	ran	run

3. *Changes to final* en, n, *or* ne *in participle.* (Changes for simple past tense are irregular.) Many of these words are changing, and on this list are some words that were once regular.

simple	*past*	*participle*
awake†	awoke, awaked	awaked, awoke, awoken
be	was/were	been
bear	bore	born, borne††
beat	beat	beaten, beat

simple	*past*	*participle*
bite	bit	bitten, bit
*blow	blew	blown
*break	broke	broken
choose	chose	chosen
*do	did	done
*draw	drew	drawn
drive	drove	driven
*eat	ate	eaten
fall	fell	fallen
*fly	flew	flown
*forbid	forbade, forbad	forbidden
forget	forgot	forgotten, forgot
forgive	forgave	forgiven
forsake	forsook	forsaken
freeze	froze	frozen
get	got	gotten, got
*give	gave	given
*go	went	gone
*grow	grew	grown
hide	hid	hidden, hid
*know	knew	known
*lie†††	lay	lain
mow	mowed	mowed, mown
prove	proved	proved, proven
*ride	rode	ridden
rise	rose	risen
*saw	sawed	sawed, sawn
*see	saw	seen
sew	sewed	sewn, sewed
*shake	shook	shaken
shave	shaved	shaved, shaven
show	showed	shown, showed
slay	slew	slain
smite	smote	smitten
sow	sowed	sown, sowed
*speak	spoke	spoken

simple	*past*	*participle*
*steal	stole	stolen
*strew	strewed	strewed, strewn
*stride	strode	stridden
strive	strove, strived	striven, strived
*swear	swore	sworn
swell	swelled	swollen, swelled
*take	took	taken
*tear	tore	torn
*throw	threw	thrown
*tread	trod, treaded	trodden, trod
wake	waked, woke	waked, woken, woke
*wear	wore	worn
weave	wove, weaved	woven, weaved
*write	wrote	written

† The verb *awaken* has one simple past tense, *awakened.*

†† *Born* is the past participle when one means *giving birth. Borne* is the past participle for the meaning *carrying.*

††† *Lie,* meaning to tell an untruth, is regular and the past form is *lied.* Here *lie* means to recline on a surface.

Catch 1: Look-Alike Verbs Trip Us Up

There are several verb couplets that seem invented to trap the unwary. We'll single them out here for special attention.

drug and *drag*—Both are regular verbs that have simple past tenses: *drug, drugged* and *drag, dragged.*

> WRONG: I have drug him home time and time again.
> CORRECT: I have dragged him home time and time again.

fall and *fell*—When something drops it *falls.* When a person makes something else drop, such as a tree, he *fells* it. *Fell* is a regular verb; its past tense is *felled.* Don't confuse it with the past tense of *fall,* which is fell.

lie and *lay*—*Lie* (*lay, lain*) means to recline on a bed or other surface. *Lay* (past tense *laid*) means to put something else on a surface. Memorize the distinction. It's often used by paper-correctors to separate the literates from the illiterates.

lose and *loose—Lose* (past tense *lost*) means misplace or fail to keep. *Loose* (past tense *loosed*) and *loosen* (past tense *loosened*) both mean untie. Memorize the correct spelling of these words. (The confusion occurs because *choose* is spelled like *loose* but pronounced like *lose*!)

lend and *loan*—Until recently, *loan* wasn't considered an acceptable verb, just a noun. Now most people use *loan* (*loaned*) and *lend* (*lent*) interchangeably in speaking. If you're writing to impress, choose *lend.*

see and *saw—Saw,* meaning cut with a saw, is often confused with *see* in its past tenses.

saw	sawed	sawed or sawn
see	saw	seen

WRONG: I seed him, I sawed him (unless you cut him up)

CORRECT: I saw him. I sawed the log.

set and *sit—Set* and *sit* used to be like *lay* and *lie, sit* meaning to put yourself down and *set* meaning to put something down. Due to definition, it's always been incorrect to say *set down,* but perfectly correct to say *set yourself down.* In many parts of the United States, the distinction is dying; however, when you're writing you're expected to keep it alive. The verb *sit* has the past tense *sat.* The verb *set* doesn't change to show past tense.

The men sat down.
The men set the book on the table.

span and *spun—Span* (*spanned*) is a verb meaning measure or form an arch over something. Once upon a time it was also the past tense of *spin* (*spun*). But it isn't considered correct in that usage any more.

rise and *raise—Rise* and *raise* are like *lay* and *lie:* you *rise* when you pick yourself up, and you *raise* when you pick up something. It's correct to say *raise yourself* but not *rise up the flag* (unless it's self-propelled). *Raise* (*raised*) is a regular verb. *Rise* (*rose, risen*) is irregular. Memorize the distinction.

passed and *past—Past* can be a noun, an adjective, an adverb, a preposition—but not a verb. The past tense of *pass* is *passed.* Check your spelling.

CLUE 2: SOME PLURAL SUBJECTS TAKE SINGULAR VERBS

Let's look again at the verb characteristic known as *person*. We mentioned previously that nearly all verbs add *-s* to show *third person singular,* the *he, she, it* form. It's usually simple to figure out whether you need the *-s:*

> The Empire State Building stands tall. (one building)
> In the Empire State, buildings stand tall. (more than one building)

Difficulties arise only when you're not sure whether the subject is singular or plural. As we saw in Chapter 1, collective nouns and uncountables are particularly hard to pin down. Which of the following is correct, for example?

> The family goes to the movies together.
> The family all sit in separate parts of the theater.
> The family is scattered throughout the theater.

All three sentences are correct. Notice how awkward it would sound to change the second sentence from plural to singular:

> The family all sits in separate parts of the theater.

In speech, we seldom worry about collective nouns and uncountables. We choose our verbs, singular or plural, sometimes according to what seems sensible, sometimes strictly according to whim. But the grammarians who tried to tidy up the language found this haphazardness deplorable, so they invented the following rule:

When the group or quantity in the subject is regarded as a unit, use the singular verb. When it's regarded as parts of a unit, or as individuals, use the plural verb.

Paper-correctors like to look for infractions of this rule, so use it whenever writing standard school English.

CLUE 3: KNOW HOW TO DEAL WITH FANCY TENSES

When the English language was new, there were only two distinct time frames, present and past. To show future you added a time indicator: *I go tomorrow. Meet me at 8 o'clock.* As you can see, some shreds of that are still left in the language. However, we now have more than a half dozen distinct tenses. Most of them are made by adding other verbs—*have, be,* or *do*—as well as words that the grammarians call *helping* or *auxiliary verbs:* can, could, may, might, must, shall, should, will, would. There are also a number of semi-auxiliaries just to complicate verbs more: ought to, get, be able to, let, go, come (as in *come to be ashamed*). These auxiliaries are always added to either the simple verb, the past participle (which was discussed in Clue 1), or the present participle, the *-ing* form of the verb. Let's look at the four most-used new tenses:

future—to show that an action will be begun and completed in the future.

FORMULA: will or shall + simple verb
EXAMPLE: I *will go*. You *will stay* here.

present perfect—to show that an action is completed but still important now.

FORMULA: have (or has) + past participle
EXAMPLE: I *have gone* there three times. He *has*n't *gone* there yet.

past perfect—to show that an action completed in the past was important in the more recent past.

FORMULA: had + past participle
EXAMPLE: By the time you arrived, I *had* already *left*.

future perfect—to show that an action will be completed in the future, but before some other action.

FORMULA: will (or shall) + have + past participle
EXAMPLE: We *shall have seen* him before you get there.

When past, present, and future tenses of the verb *be* are used with the present participle, grammarians call them *progressive* verbs. They, too, show tense changes:

I *was speaking* to him at the time.
I *am speaking* to him now.
I *will be speaking* to him some time soon.

In addition, you can link together all the verb forms and the many auxiliaries to show all sorts of subtle variations:

I should have been going there.
I may have been able to have gone there.
He let me be able to be going there tomorrow.

Some of these variations in tense are so hard to distinguish from one another, we almost never use them in speech. But in writing reports, speeches, and instructions, it is often helpful to be able to make skillful use of them. They not only make for more precision of meaning, but vary sentences that might otherwise sound monotonous.

Catch 2: *Shall* Isn't Dead Yet

In England, there's a difference in meaning between *shall* and *will,* and grammarians have tried to keep that distinction here in America. You may have learned a rule about their use in school. If you follow the rule, nobody will mark you wrong. But most of today's American dictionaries agree that *shall* is being dropped from American speech and writing. Even in questions, it's disappearing, *should* being substituted:

> Shall I go or shall we?
> Should I go or should we?

It's safe to say that no sensible paper-corrector will mark you wrong if you stick to *will* and forget about *shall.*

CLUE 4: TRANSLATE SPEECH PROPERLY TO PAPER

When we speak, we streamline the language, leaving out sounds that aren't needed to make the meaning clear. Much of the streamlining has concentrated on the common verbs *have* and *be* and the pronouns that often accompany them. On paper these shorthand phrases are written as *contractions,* with apostrophes inserted to show where sounds have been omitted. People who haven't done much careful reading sometimes spell or use these contractions wrong in their writing. We have provided a list to check against.

Correcting Spoken Contractions

Spoken contraction	Full meaning of contraction	Example of correct written use of contraction
*I'd†	I had, I would	(Had) I'd already done that. (Would) I'd like to do that.
*I'll	I will	I'll be leaving soon.
*I'd've (or I'd'of)	I would have	I'd have gone there first.
*I've	I have	I've spent six pence.
I'm	I am	I'm happy to see you.
you'd, you'll, you'd've, you've		(See "*" entries above)
you're	you are	You're doing just fine.
he'd, he'll, he'd've (same for she . . . , it. . . .)		(See "I" entries above)
he's	he is	He's an "A" student.
we'd, we'll, we'd've (same for they. . . .)		(See "*" entries above.)
**won't	will not	They won't do it.
**wouldn't	would not	They wouldn't try it.
**won't've	will not have	He won't have gone yet.
**wouldn't've	would not have	I wouldn't have done it that way.
**won't'of	will not have	He won't have gone yet.
**wouldn't'of	would not have	I wouldn't have done it that way.
(**same for can, could, should)		
who'd†	who had, who would	(Had) Who'd gone to bed? (Would) Who'd buy that?
who'll	who will	Who'll buy my car?
who's†	who is, who has	(Is) Who's going? (Has) Who's taken my pen?
who'd've	who would have	Who'd have guessed he was the one?
there's†	there is, there has	(Is) There's no chance. (Has) There's been a change.
there'd†	there had, there would	(Had) There'd been a change. (Would) There'd be no chance.

† Notice that some contractions can have two meanings. Be sure to translate correctly contractions such as I'd (I had or I would), who'd, who's, there's, there'd. Also, be sure not to confuse *they're* with *their*, *there's* with *theirs*, *who's* with *whose*.

As you can see from the list on page 45, *I's, youse,* and *they's* are not contractions for anything in standard English, whether written or spoken. Avoid them unless you're among good friends.

Many teachers consider contractions too informal for serious writing. Since they sometimes cause spelling problems anyway, sidestep them unless you're writing dialogue.

CLUE 5: PASSIVE HAS ITS PLACE

Passive voice is the grammarians' term for what you do to a verb when you don't want to show its subject, or prefer to mention the object first. Using passive is easy once you understand the formula: convert the verb to its *past participle* (for example, *draw* becomes drawn) and add *be* or *become* or *get* in the tense you've just eliminated. (In present tense, we usually add the progressive verb *being*.)

ACTIVE PRESENT: He draws the picture.
PASSIVE PRESENT: The picture is being drawn.
ACTIVE PAST: He drew the picture.
PASSIVE PAST: The picture got drawn.
ACTIVE FUTURE: He will draw the picture.
PASSIVE FUTURE: The picture will be drawn.

Our sentences are usually clearer and more forceful when we avoid passive voice. But it's useful when we don't know who's done whatever-it-is, or don't think our readers need to know.

Catch 3: The Prejudice Against *get*

In modern spoken English, *get* is used more often than *be* or *become* to show passive voice:

ACTIVE: The boss fired John.
PASSIVE: John got fired.

But many schoolteachers turn their noses up at *get,* considering it a substandard helping verb. When you're writing to impress, it's best to switch to *be* or *become:*

PASSIVE: John was fired.

CLUE 6: A VERB IS SOMETIMES A TWO-WORD UNIT

Most grammar books duck the untidy fact that a large number of English verbs are two or three words long, made up of a root verb and one or more prepositions tacked on at the end. The new verbs have very different meanings from their verb roots, and some have several distinct meanings themselves. Here's one example, showing all the words we've created using *come.*

come—move toward something, approach
come about—happen, change direction
come along—accompany
come across—pay over money, meet, produce an impression
come back—return to memory, reply
come between—cause to be estranged
come by—make a visit
come down—become ill, fall in condition, pass on by tradition
come in—arrive, become available, place among finishers as in a race
come into—acquire
come on—begin by degrees, project a certain image
come over—change sides, seize suddenly
come round, come around—change direction, return to a former condition, accede

come through—do what's needed
come to—recover consciousness, bring a ship's head nearer the wind
come up—approach, rise in status, occur in time
come up on—approach suddenly
come upon—meet

It's important to know a two-word verb when you hear or see one, because sometimes separating the components destroys your meaning:

The woman hit her head and *came to* on the floor.
The woman hit her head and *came* on *to* the floor.
The duke *came by* to see me yesterday.
The duke *came* to see me *by* yesterday.

The previous two-word verbs are *intransitive. Transitive* multi-word verbs, those that take direct objects, sometimes permit you to insert a short object between the verb and its preposition part. Here are the rules:

1. *Pronoun* objects should *always* be inserted, unless you want to emphasize the pronoun:

The man *called* me *up* the other day.
The man *called up* me the other day.

2. Short objects can be inserted or not:

The man *called* his mother *up*.
The man *called up* his mother.

3. Long multi-word objects should *never* be inserted.

The man *called up* the person who was next in line.

NOT:

The man *called* the person who was next in line *up*.

It's this confusion over splitting two-word verbs that caused grammarians to invent the silly rule that we must never end a sentence with a preposition. As you can see from the pronoun example, the rule is downright wrong. (For more on this, see page 90.)

CLUE 7: SOME VERBS TAKE SPECIAL PREPOSITIONS

The two-word verbs discussed above *always* have different meanings from the one-word verbs at their root. Most of them are listed and defined as words in any good dictionary. In addition, many one- and two-word verbs always appear linked with one or two special prepositions. The prepositions don't change the verb's meaning, but have by custom become the only correct prepositions to follow these particular verbs when used to introduce certain specific ideas. Unfortunately, we've discovered no dictionary that shows the correct prepositions to use with particular verbs to express particular meanings. You'll just have to acquire an ear and an eye for what seems correct. Here are some examples of what we mean.

look at—used when there's a specific direct object
look on, look upon—when there's no direct object specifically in the subject's sight

EXAMPLES: He looked *on* the venture with disfavor.
He looked *at* that venture with disfavor.

collapse on—fall onto an object
collapse in a particular way

EXAMPLE: She collapsed *in* a heap.

come through for someone
come through with something

EXAMPLES: I asked for a pen and he came through for me.
I asked for a pen and he came through with one.

We *extricate* ourselves *from* a particular situation, not *out of* or *off* or *of*. We are *bludgeoned with* a weapon, not *by* or *from*. A plant is *composed of* several parts, not *out of*. These verb-preposition groups, and many others, cause papers to be returned to students with *awk* scrawled all over the margins.

Catch 4: The Split Infinitive Has Not Yet Won Its Battle

The *infinitive* is the simple present form of the verb with the word *to* in front of it. In this case, *to* doesn't mean *into* or *toward;* it's just a filler that connects the upcoming verb with a previous verb, or that changes the verb into a noun.

VERB CONNECTOR: He wants to go there. (*wants* and *go* are verbs)
NOUN INDICATOR: To write means to struggle. (*means* is the only verb)

One of the rules the old grammarians made up out of whole cloth was the following: never split an infinitive. In other words, they said, never separate *to* from the verb that follows it. Although it's perfectly correct to write:

He always *arrives* at school promptly.

they tell us it is wrong to write:

To always *arrive* at school promptly is a crime.

The fact is, spoken English splits infinitives all the time. The alternatives are so rarely used, they often sound awkward:

> Always to arrive at school promptly is a crime.
> To arrive always at school promptly is a crime.

Modern experts even suggest that the verb connector *to* really belongs with the previous verb, not the following one, and that's why we all say:

> I agreed to carefully set the book on the table.

NOT:

> I agreed to set carefully the book on the table.

So don't split hairs over split infinitives unless you're writing for an eighteenth-century holdover.

CLUE 8: MOOD IS A SOMETIME THING

Like so many other terms in grammar, *mood* in grammar has nothing to do with *mood* in real life. The word came from *mode,* meaning *way*. In English grammar, *mood* refers to the way in which a listener or reader should react to the verb. The three moods used by most old-fashioned grammarians, in terms they often use to define them, are:

INDICATIVE MOOD:	used in a sentence or question
IMPERATIVE MOOD:	for commands, instructions, and requests
SUBJUNCTIVE MOOD:	for wishes or contrary-to-fact ideas, and for *that* clauses of recommendation or request

Since few people have any difficulty writing in the first two moods, even when they don't know the grammatical names for what they're doing, we'll concentrate on the mood that does cause problems: the subjunctive. The reason it's hard to use correctly is that it's disappearing from spoken English.

	indicative mood	*subjunctive mood*
VERB *be:*	I am, was	I be, were
	you are, were	you be, were
	he is, was	he be, were
	we are, were	we be, were
	they are, were	they be, were
VERB *do:*	he does	he do

Nowadays, we find other ways of saying the same thing:

I asked *that he do* this. (subjunctive)
I asked if he would do this. (transitional)
I asked him to do this. (common indicative)

In fact, the only still-common use of the subjunctive is in expressions like *If I were you . . .* Even that's changing slowly, in speech, to *If I was you.* However, in standard written English (and in formal speaking) this newer form is considered illiterate.

CHECKUP QUIZ

1. In the following paragraph, underline each verb and correct it if it's incorrectly written.

After class I lay my books on the table and set myself down on a chair that I drug up alongside it. All at once I seen a paper laying there that I'd swore I give to my sister the day before. She'd probably hope to hide it from me, because it look like it was tore. I had rather she'd of told me. Next time I loan something to her, she better not rip it up and then try to squirrel it out of sight. I wouldn't of loaned it to her in the first place if I'd of known that she'd gotten unable to take care of things.

2. Insert the correct word.

a. We ______ get there some time tomorrow. (shall, will)
b. I ______ go to school anymore. (shan't, won't)
c. On the last hike, nobody ______ lost. (got, became, was)
d. The gentleman threatened to beat him ______ the next county. (to, into, up to)
e. The gentleman threatened to beat him ______. (to, in, up)
f. The gentleman threatened to beat him ______ a pulp. (to, into, up to)
g. A number of letters ______ written by the boy. (was, were)
h. I ______ him one candy but the remainder ______ lost. (gave, give; are, is)
i. Everybody ______ in line at once. (get, gets)
j. Either of the boys ______ (is, are) responsible for the damage.
k. I wouldn't move if I ______ the last man on Earth. (was, were)
l. Come ______ to my place and we'll listen to music. (on, up)

3. In the paragraph excerpted on page 16, circle every verb.

4
MODIFIERS

A modifier is a word or phrase put into a sentence to make the meaning of another word or phrase clearer or more precise. In short, it describes. It usually answers the question *how, how much, when, why, which,* or *where.* (Notice that it doesn't answer the question *what:* the subject and object do that.)

If the modifier modifies a noun, it's called an adjective. Generally if it modifies anything else, it's called an adverb. If several modifiers in a row come before a noun, the one just before the noun is definitely an adjective. The others are adjectives only if they directly affect the noun, in which case we usually separate them with commas.

EXAMPLE: The *heavy, red, expensive* truck drove by.

However, if the earlier words modify the adjective just before the noun, then they're adverbs.

EXAMPLE: The quick, tawny brown fox jumped over
adj. adv. adj. n. vb.
the lazy, fat dog.
adj. adj. n.

Notice how we separated the adjectives from other adjectives and adverb–adjective phrases with commas. In the above example, some grammarians might quibble over calling *tawny* an adverb. But since it's used to modify *brown* and not *fox,* it acts like an adverb.

In English, unlike many languages, we rarely put adjectives after their nouns. When we do, it sounds literary or poetic.

> Make a noise joyous and loud.
> n. adj. adj.
>
> Let's dance the light fantastic.
> n. adj.

Modifiers of verbs, on the other hand, may precede or follow the verb, but generally follow if they're more than one or two words long.

> The boy steps slowly and carefully into view.
> vb. adv. adv.

In fact, if there's an object in the sentence, the adverbs often shift to follow the object.

> The boy runs all the way to school very quickly.
> vb. adv. adv.

Because of the primary rule of English—that it's not a specific word, but its placement in the sentence, that determines its part of speech—almost any word, phrase, or clause can be used as an adverb:

NOUN USED AS ADVERB:	Let's go *home.*
PHRASE USED AS ADVERB:	He talks *without stopping.*
CLAUSES USED AS ADVERBS:	The fox *with the black spot over one eye* ran *after the hunter shot his arrow.* (The first clause is an adjective clause showing *which* fox, the second an adverb clause showing *when.)*

Few one-word modifiers cause trouble in speaking or writing. Let's concentrate on the ones that do.

CLUE 1: *-LY* WORDS ARE NOT ALWAYS ADVERBS, AND ADVERBS ARE NOT ALWAYS *-LY* WORDS

Some of our worst difficulties with English grammar arise because we've been taught that most adjectives can be turned into adverbs by adding *-ly*. This is true for many adjectives.

adjective	*adverb*
adverbial	adverbially
troublesome	troublesomely
characteristic	characteristically

But the rule is an oversimplification, and we can clear it up by going back to Old English.

In Old English, one way of forming both adjectives and adverbs was by adding the word *like* to a noun or adjective. In Modern English, *-like* has been shortened to *-ly,* and two groups of *-ly* words are still much used today: adjectives that come from nouns and our old friends, adverbs that come from adjectives.

noun	*Old English adjective*	*Modern adjective*
man	manlike	manly
time	timelike	timely
friend	friendlike	friendly

adjective	*Old English adverb*	*Modern adverb*
blunt	bluntlike	bluntly
kind	kindlike	kindly
rough	roughlike	roughly

In addition, there are still some holdovers from two other groups: adverbs based on nouns (he treats me *friendly*), which are nowadays considered illiterate and should be avoided in standard school English; and adjectives based on other adjectives (a *goodly* portion, a *kindly* appearance), which are fading fast from our language.

But there was another way of forming adverbs from adjectives in Old English: by adding *-e* to the adjective:

wid, wide	long, longe

Eventually one form, usually the one without the *-e*, became standard for both the adjective and adverb. Today these words include *hard, long, fast, strong, full, wide, weak, high, thick, soft, far, near, steady.*

adjective	*adverb*
a *near* miss	come *near*
a *steady* hand	stand *steady*

Most of these words occur as adverbs in phrases so old, they're idiomatic. As phrases, they rarely cause trouble.

easy come, easy go
mighty kind
clean through
sure enough
wide apart
going strong
full well
straight from the shoulder
think hard
fly high
sleep late

The trouble is, the more *-ly* has become the mark of an adverb, the harder it's been for people to keep from sticking

-ly on these old adverbs. Folks are beginning to "correct" some and to confuse others. They've made new words by adding *-ly,* and some have been accepted.

rest quiet(ly)
go slow(ly)
feel bad(ly)

But others are still considered substandard by strict grammarians:

speak ill (not *illy*)

These grammarians also want to see you keep a distinction between the following words:

adjective	*adverb*
sure	surely
real	really
awful	awfully

He surely does make a loud noise. (not *sure*)
It gets really warm in the summer. (not *real*)

It's especially tricky to know whether you've got an adjective or adverb when it comes between the verb and a noun. You must stop and consider which word is being modified.

To complicate matters, there's a group of about 60 verbs called *linking verbs* that take *adjectives* instead of adverbs. These are the verbs that show some form of existence (be, get, keep, work, become, stay, hold, remain, appear, etc.) and verbs of the senses (see, taste, sound, look, etc.)

non-linking	*linking*
He jumps *quietly*.	He looks *quiet*.
The knife cuts *sharply*.	The knife feels *sharp*.
He *surely* makes a loud noise.	It *sure* gets warm sometimes.

As you can see from the last example, you've got to keep your eye out for those linking verbs when you're choosing between two forms of the same modifier. To add to the confusion, the verbs of the senses change to non-linking verbs when they're showing active participation.

LINKING: The water feels *deep.*
NON-LINKING: The boy feels *deeply.*
LINKING: The flute sounds *sweet.*
NON-LINKING: He sounds his flute *sweetly* for us.

How can you make sure to use the correct word? Even the cleverest of us sometimes get tripped up. The best way is to listen to educated speakers and read well-written books. Steep yourself in standard school English.

Catch 1: *good* and *well, bad* and *badly*

These words are trickier than almost any others in the language. That's because *bad* is, almost without exception, an adjective.

WITH LINKING VERB: I feel bad. (My health or emotions are low.)
WITH NOUN: the bad boy

But *badly, good,* and *well* can be either adjective or adverb.

ADJECTIVE WITH NOUN: a good boy (behaves ok)
a well man (not sick)
ADJECTIVE WITH LINKING VERB: I feel well. (in good health)
I feel bad about that. (unpleasant emotion)

ADVERB WITH NON-LINKING VERB: I feel well. (My sense of touch is good.)
I feel badly. (My sense of touch is poor.)

The only way to keep these words straight is to memorize their meanings, as demonstrated above.

CLUE 2: WHICH COMPARISONS USE *-ER, -EST*; AND WHICH USE *MORE* AND *MOST*

Adjectives and adverbs both have a quality that grammar books call *degree of comparison.* We use it whenever unequal actions or things are compared. (When they're equal, we use *as . . . as:* I'm as good as they are.) The *comparative* degree shows relative value, and is usually formed by adding *-er, more,* or *less;* the *superlative* degree is usually formed by adding *-est, most,* or *least.* (Don't confuse this use of *most* with its idiomatic use: the boy was *most* cordial to me. There it just means *very.*)

By and large, one-syllable adjectives and adverbs add *-er* and *-est,* while words of more than one syllable use *more* and *most.* Two-syllable words ending in *-y* sometimes change the *-y* to *i* and tack on the appropriate ending. However, these words also may instead be used with *more* and *most;* generally either alternative is correct.

busy	busier	busiest
	more busy	most busy

Words that end in *-ly* rarely change the *-y* to *i.*

	friendly	friendlier	friendliest
BUT:			
	loudly	more loudly	most loudly

Here, your ear must be your guide.

Only a few words are irregular in forming degree of comparison. Here are the most common.

good	better	best
well	better	best
bad	worse	worst
badly	worse	worst
many	more	most
much	more	most
little	less	least
far {	farther	farthest
	further	furthest

Notice that *worser* is not an English word, even though it's tempting to add the *-r*. Also note that there is no difference in meaning between *farther* and *further* or *farthest* and *furthest,* contrary to what you may read in outdated grammar books.

Catch 2: Some Words Can't Be Compared

Such words as *unique, perfect, perfectly, square, round, absolute,* and *supremely* contain implication of *the most* in their meanings. One thing cannot be more perfect or unique than another. If you need to show comparison using such qualities, choose instead *more nearly:* more nearly perfect, more nearly square, more nearly unique.

WRONG: This is the most unique hairstyle I've ever seen.
MORE ACCURATE: This is the most nearly unique hairstyle . . .
EVEN BETTER: This is the cleverest hairstyle . . .

Catch 3: Watch the Pronouns that Follow Comparisons

When it comes to choosing a pronoun to follow a comparison, spoken English takes the easy way out, while grammarians have tried to counter our changing language with a strict rule.

In colloquial English, comparisons of verbs often take objective pronouns.

She does it better than me.
vb. adj. pro.

The grammar rule is: After comparisons, use the subjective case of the pronoun since a noun phrase is implied.

She does it better than I. (better than *I do it)*

This is the rule most teachers have learned, so you'd be wise to adhere to it in writing standard school English. But in *all* your writing, you must select the subjective if using the objective will confuse your meaning.

He likes her as much as I. (as much as I like her)
He likes her as much as me. (as much as he likes me)

CLUE 3: DON'T USE SHORTHAND IN COMPARING

In speaking, we often leave out reference to one of the things we're comparing. We assume that our listeners know what we're talking about.

The bigger boy (of the two boys) took the prize.
Our pool is bigger than the YMCA ('s pool).

When the comparison modifies a noun, as in the first example above, it's perfectly correct to omit mention of the other thing being compared, even in writing, because it's clearly suggested by the noun that *is* mentioned. As you can see, the first sentence above is clear when we omit the words in parentheses.

But in making comparisons that modify a verb, the meaning may be misunderstood unless we insert every reference to what's being compared. As the second example above shows, dropping the words in parentheses changes the sentence's meaning.

Because there's so much room for misunderstanding, it's a good rule—and one most careful writers insist on—to always state *both* elements in a comparison unless you're comparing nouns.

CLUE 4: CLEAR UP THE *THAN/THEN* CONFUSION

In speaking, *than* and *then* are pronounced so similarly that it's hard for a listener to know which one is being said. Since we've learned English by listening, it's not surprising that sometimes the wrong word is chosen in writing. The best way to stay out of trouble is to memorize the various uses of each word.

THAN

1. *Than* (not *then*) is always used when comparing modifiers.

> I am not better than anyone else.

2. *Than* is also used to show a difference in kind, manner, or identity, as in the expressions *other than* and *rather than* (though *but* is often substituted by writers who want to avoid trouble).

Don't go anywhere else than home.

If you can mentally or physically substitute *other than* or *rather than,* it will clue you in to the correct spelling.

3. *Than* is used after some words, especially *scarcely, barely,* and *hardly,* to mean *when.*

Scarcely had I awoken than the phone rang.

If you're not sure of the spelling in this case, substitute *when.*

THEN

1. *Then* is used to mean *at that time,* or to mean *following soon after in time, position, or in a series of any kind.*

Then the door burst open.
First came the footmen, then the horsemen.
The then secretary of state signed the bill.

2. *Then* is used, often surrounded by commas, to mean *in that case, according to that,* or *as it appears.*

Take it, then, if you need it so much.
Is your mind made up, then?

3. *Then* is used after *but* to qualify the preceding statement.

He lost, but then he never expected to win.

4. *Then* is used with *if* to mean *as a result.*

If you're silly, then I'll stop talking to you.

Notice that *than* is never part of an *if* statement.

CLUE 5: OTHER MODIFIERS THAT TRIP THE UNWARY

There are several sets of modifiers that seem created to cause writing errors. Most of the errors can be avoided easily once you know what to watch for.

kind of, sort of, and **equally**—In speaking, we often insert the word *a* after the phrases *kind of* and *sort of,* and the word *as* after *equally.* In standard written English, these colloquialisms are considered illiterate. If the extra word creeps in, delete it from your writing.

different from—The modifier *different* classically takes the preposition *from.* In speaking, many of us say *different than,* but the idiom is still substandard in school English.

WRONG: This book is different *than* that.
CORRECT: This book is different *from* that.

this/these, that/those—One set of adjectives that answers the question *which* is: *this, these, that,* and *those.* They are called indicators. Everyone recognizes that *this* is used when referring to *one* noun and *these* when referring to more than one; *that* refers to one and *those* to several. *This* and *these* are nearby; *that* and *those* are not nearby. In general, we select the correct word automatically.

But we have trouble choosing between singular and plural when it's not clear whether the noun in question is singular or plural. This is particularly true when a grammatically singular noun refers to a group and the sentence contains a modifying phrase naming the group more specifically. The rule is, the noun after the indicator determines its number, not the noun in the modifying phrase.

WRONG: These type of people are hard to deal with.
CORRECT: This type of people is hard to deal with.

Notice that if you mentally delete the modifying phrase (*of people* in the above example) you'll not only get your indicator correct, but your verb as well.

We also sometimes have trouble choosing between singular and plural indicator when the noun is collective or uncountable. In this case, too, the form of the noun determines the form of the indicator.

> Some of this grass is wet.
> Some of these grasses are brown and some are green.

Again, make sure you also have the correct form of the verb.

The number of the noun in the sentence's modifying phrase can't always be counted on to show which indicator you need. Either of the following is correct.

> I want those sorts of cake for my party.
> I want those sorts of cakes for my party.

The plural noun *cakes* not only shows several cakes rather than one, it also makes the noun much more tangible.

But while we can say *I want that sort of cake, I want that sort of cakes* is grammatically incorrect. In general, awareness and common sense will lead you to the correct choice.

this here, that there—The commonly spoken idioms *this here* and *that there* are considered incorrect in standard school English, even though they're acceptable when separated by one or more words.

> CORRECT: That house over there is for sale.
> WRONG: That there house is for sale.

To correct, delete the word *there.*

them for **those** and **these**—In many places, *them* is incorrectly substituted for *those* and *these* in speaking. The mistake comes from extending a proper use of the pronoun *them.*

CORRECT: I don't want any of them.
WRONG: I don't want any of them apples.
CORRECT: I don't want any of those apples.

Keep in mind that *them* is a pronoun. It can't be used as a modifier. Even in speaking, this usage is wrong.

modifiers with and without -s—The modifier *backward* has been slowly changing to *backwards,* until now the dictionary considers both equally correct. The modifier *besides* changed from *beside* a long time ago; now, we're told, *beside* is only correct when used as a preposition (to mean *at the side of* or *on a par with*), while *besides* can be either preposition (meaning *other than* or *in addition to*) or modifier.

Sometime has been changing to *sometimes;* at this point the two words coexist with slightly different meanings. It's not surprising that *somewheres* and its companions *anywheres* and *nowheres* have been creeping into spoken English too. But these variations are still considered substandard, so avoid them when you write.

CHECKUP QUIZ

1. In the following paragraph, circle all the adjectives and adverbs, marking them *adj.* or *adv.*

The world's most talented sleuths are racing to track down a ferocious killer that strikes victims with such great intensity, their brains are totally reduced to a spongy pulp. The assailant has left behind a tangled trail of death and destruction from the steamy jungles of New Guinea to the sheep ranches of America. Here is a medical detective story that certainly contains all the most lovely elements of the best science-fiction thrillers.

2. Correct the following sentences.

a. The awful question is whether television will continue to satisfy these sort of people.
b. Don't miss out on this here opportunity since its your last chance.
c. When I got this here boat, it sure reminded them of them sails hid away over there.
d. He just sat there staring blank at the screen, wanting bad to get up and go somewheres else.
e. It sure is mighty kind of you to sweat so mightily in my behalf.
f. He kept an awful chilly silence under the still, lonely moon, though they sure tried hard and mightily to make him yell out.
g. This sure has been the most coldest day of the year.
h. I'm surely going to be more near perfect the next time I try this crummy exercise.
i. Broadcasting is the most persuasive means of communication ever known, and even more entertaining.
j. This ring is even more unique then that one.
k. He's the likeliest candidate for the job, but she's the more likely to get it.
l. Nobody wants it more badly then him.
m. Hardly had he picked up the lonely pup then the phone rang.
n. This might explain why it can lie dormantly for a few months, and then spring to life instantaneously.
o. If she hadn't looked so sweet and sunny, then I wouldn't have behaved so evilly.
p. This trip wasn't any different than the last, except that the natives spoke different and the guide wore different clothes.
q. In this case, I'm not any worser off than him.

5
SENTENCES

If you've read the King James translation of the Bible, the first thing that you noticed was all the *ands:* And bring hither the fatted calf, and kill it, and let us eat and be merry. . . . The reason for all the *ands* is that Biblical Hebrew was made up entirely of just simple sentences (subject + verb + simple object) and of the simplest *compound* sentences, which are simple sentences strung together with words like *and, but, or, nor, yet, so, for.*

Old English was similar to Biblical Hebrew, in that it had *ands* and *buts* and some *either . . . ors,* but *complex* sentences didn't come into English until the Romans invaded England bringing their complex Latin language. Even some of the more complicated *compound* sentences are relative newcomers to English.

Why bother to learn complicated sentence structures, which bring all sorts of writing problems in their wake? Because they're the only way we have to adequately show the complicated relationships between ideas that most of us must deal with when we're writing reports and other business and school papers.

Most compound and complex sentences are strung together with the parts of speech called *conjunctions.* Though the special problems of some conjunctions will be discussed in the next chapter, we'll name some conjunctions here along with the relationships they show.

CLUE 1: COMPOUND SENTENCES SHOW RELATED AND EQUALLY IMPORTANT THOUGHTS

One reason to write a compound sentence is to show that a special relationship exists between the two or more simple sentences that it's composed of. The most common relationship is *equality,* and some conjunctions that show equality are *and, but, for, nor, yet, so, either.* Here is a compound sentence.

There are too few of them and too many of us.

This compound sentence expresses two equally important thoughts: There are too few of them and, equally important, there are too many of us.

Recently, a new kind of equality has been introduced into the compound sentence: *equality in sequence.* Some words that show this are *however, therefore, moreover, nevertheless, consequently, furthermore.* Until very recently, these words weren't used to join two ideas in one sentence, but to begin a new sentence. Now they still can be used that way (nearly always followed by a comma).

He's here. Furthermore, he's got his bike with him.

Or the period in the previous sentence can be changed to a semicolon to create two semi-sentences.

He's here; furthermore, he's got his bike with him.

Or one sentence can be created, often inserting *and* before the conjunction of sequence and deleting the comma after it.

He's here, and furthermore he's got his bike with him.

CLUE 2: MAKE SURE YOUR COMPOUND SENTENCES DO THE RIGHT JOB

Choose a compound sentence only when your ideas are really closely related to one another and of equal importance, and then make sure that you're showing the relationship you want shown.

> WRONG: Television is sometimes used by people as an escape from the hard cold realities of daily life, and moreover I'd love to be able to solve problems as quickly as they do on TV.

At first glance the two ideas in the above example seem closely related. But notice: (1) The subject of the first part is *people* (people use television) while the subject of the second part is *I* (I'd love to), and (2) the relationship isn't sequential: the second idea doesn't follow after the first in any sequence. If anything, the writer may be suggesting a *causal* relationship: Because people (or *I*) can't solve problems in real life as quickly as they do on television, TV is sometimes used (by *me* or by people) as an escape. A causal relationship requires a complex sentence, not a compound one.

The only way to guard against errors of this kind is to read your sentences carefully and make sure they say what you want them to say.

> CORRECT: Television is sometimes used by people as an escape from the hard cold realities of daily life, and sometimes as an electronic baby-sitter.

CLUE 3: COMPLEX SENTENCES SHOW COMPLICATED RELATIONSHIPS BETWEEN IDEAS

A complex sentence is a wonderful invention of modern writers. With it, you can economically string together many separate pieces of information that used to take many sentences to explain. The only proviso is that all the information pertain to the same topic. The conjunctions that are used to connect the pieces have been borrowed from adverbs and pronouns, and often they do double duty in a sentence as conjunction + adverb or conjunction + pronoun. Some of these new conjunctions are *who, what, which, because, since, for, so that, why, in order that, if, unless, even though, whether, as, as if, although, when, then, while, till, after, as long as, before, where, wherever, whereon.* An easy way to recognize these words and the subordinate clauses they introduce is to remember that they all answer the questions *who, which, when, where, how,* and *why* (but not *what*).

Every complex sentence is built on the backbone of an idea that can stand alone. It's called the *independent* clause. All the other information, like ribs or leg bones, attaches by way of *dependent* or *subordinate* clauses. Twentieth-century grammar innovators refer to the process of depositing information into subordinate clauses as *imbedding,* and it's an apt term for the way our minds stick in these extra ideas.

The words *independent* and *subordinate* have fooled many grammar students. The independent clause doesn't have to go at the beginning of a sentence, and the subordinate clause is only grammatically subordinate. Usually, writers put into the independent clauses the information that's most familiar to readers. Then, into their subordinate clauses, they fit the new, less familiar, or most vital *qualifiers:* the information (sometimes called *limiters* in grammar books) that actually expands the reader's understanding of the main thought. A mark of educated writing is its correct use of complex sentences, simply because only in that way can a person express complicated ideas. So for the quality papers that impress graders and bosses, it's important to acquire skill in complex sentence writing.

Independent clauses make sense when you delete the rest of the sentence. Subordinate clauses don't. Here's a famous sentence filled with subordinate clauses.

> If you are lucky enough to have lived in Paris as a young man, then wherever you go for the rest of your life, it stays with you, for Paris is a movable feast.

What's the subject of Hemingway's sentence? *Paris.* What's the independent clause? *It* (meaning Paris) *stays with you.* All the other phrases explain *when* it stays, *where* it stays, and *why* it stays. Do you have to be able to tell all this to write a good complex sentence? Not really. Just keep in mind the six words *who, which, when, where, how,* and *why,* and check your sentences against them to see if you've included only information that answers the questions about your sentence topic.

CLUE 4: SENTENCE FRAGMENTS DON'T FULLY ANSWER QUESTIONS

In speaking, we often use shorthand pieces of sentences to answer or elaborate on a point.

> OTHER PERSON: Why did he go?
> US: Because he wanted to see his father.

In writing, these incomplete sentences are labeled *sentence fragments.* If they leave out vital information needed by the reader to understand what we're saying, they're *always* wrong. If the meaning is clear, they're sometimes permitted by more relaxed grammar instructors.

One error that most often creeps into writing is the *because* fragment. Independent clauses never begin with *because, since, as, for, to, in order to, so,* or any of the other causal conjunctions. These words always flag subordinate clauses, so make sure that any sentence beginning with one of these words also includes an independent clause.

> Because he wanted to see his father, he went there.

An alternative in writing standard school English is to delete the conjunction, rewriting the sentence.

> He went there to see his father.

CLUE 5: KEEP VERB TENSES STRAIGHT IN COMPLEX SENTENCES

In the long string of thoughts that often makes up a compound or complex sentence, the time frame often shifts.

> I injected the mouse with poison and now he's dead.
> Because I injected the mouse with poison, he's now dead.

It's important to make sure that your verb tenses show the correct relative time of occurrence of the various clauses in your sentence.

> WRONG: This is his most prized cup, being given him for winning the tournament.
> CORRECT: This is his most prized cup, having been given him for winning the tournament.

A converse of this rule is never to shift tenses within a sentence *unless* you're showing a change in time frame. It confuses the reader.

WRONG: When I would go to school, I took my lunch.
CORRECT: When I would go to school, I would take my lunch.
When I went to school, I took my lunch.

As you can see from the above examples, you may find yourself using some fancy tenses in your writing. If you can't already juggle them with ease, start practicing. If you try, instead, to avoid them, your writing ends up sounding superficial and unintelligent.

CLUE 6: KEEP THE SUBJECT FROM SHIFTING WITHIN ITS SENTENCE

A compound sentence may have many subjects, since by definition it's a string of independent sentences. When we speak, we sometimes shift subjects even in complex sentences. Notice the following shift from *a person* to *you.*

> A person can be a lot more pleasant if you don't have to put up with crying children.

Grammarians call this shift *lack of agreement* and expect you to avoid it in standard written English. It most often slips in nowadays in an attempt to avoid using the awkward *his or her* and a refusal to opt for just *his.* A better solution is to revise the sentence, if you can do it quickly without changing your meaning. Here's one revision of the previous sentence.

Pleasantness comes easier when crying children aren't within earshot.

CLUE 7: COMPLEX SENTENCES HAVE A GENERAL PHRASE ORDER

When you're talking about something, your listener usually wants to know the details in the following order: *when and where, how,* and then *why*. The same thing is generally true in writing. When you're putting together a complex sentence, it helps to assemble your various phrases and clauses in either of the following orders:

where, when, how, why
when, where, how, why

Here's an example from a recent periodical.

An American doctor stumbled onto the path of the deadly particle while vacationing in New Guinea with friends.

There are many exceptions to this general guideline. But if you've written a sentence that sounds ineffective, try turning it around to fit this suggested general order.

Sometimes choosing the wrong order can change a sensible idea into a silly sentence.

WRONG: I heard that he had been shot on the radio.
CORRECT: I heard on the radio that he had been shot.

Careful rereading of your written words will help you find these errors.

CLUE 8: KEEP ADVERBS AND ADJECTIVES IN THE RIGHT CLAUSE

Sometimes, in speech, we insert a long clause or phrase between an adjective or an adverb and the word it modifies.

> I knew the man who'd been shot personally.

In writing, that construction is called a *dangling* modifier. Instead of staying right with its verb, the word *personally* dangles at the end of the sentence. It's considered incorrect by all but the laxest grammarians, and should be shifted to its correct place in the sentence.

> I knew personally the man who'd been shot.

If a misplaced modifier sits in the midst of a sentence, not clearly belonging to one clause or another, it's called a *squinting* modifier. Some wag named it that because it "squints" in several directions at once.

> SQUINTER: Students who can type *normally* are put into advanced classes.

The best way to handle a squinter is to rewrite the sentence.

> Normally, students who can type are put into . . .
> Students with normal typing abilities are put into . . .

Phrases, not just single words, can be squinters.

> SQUINTER: Camping at the seashore *in the last few days* has been my favorite activity.
>
> BETTER: In the last few days, camping at the seashore has been my favorite activity.
>
> OR: My favorite activity has been the last few days of camping at the seashore.

The best way to write coherent complex sentences is not to look for squinters and danglers and incorrect phrase order, but to write your sentences and then take time to revise them so that they say exactly what you mean in the clearest terms possible. Use these clues and crutches only if all else fails.

CHECKUP QUIZ

1. The following passages, taken from books for children, use only the simplest sentence structure. With only the information contained in each passage, rewrite, using complex sentences, so that they sound like they were written for adults.

a. The sled hit a bump.
Bob and Ben fell from the sled.
The little sled did not stop.
It ran on and on.
It ran into a red barn.
The barn bent the little sled.
And the sled dented the barn.
Bob and Ben got wet.

b. Every day we see and hear a great deal of advertising. The words and pictures on our box of breakfast cereal are advertising. Our carton of milk usually has advertising on it. The commercial we hear on radio and both see and hear on television is also advertising. So are most of the circulars our mailman brings.

Newspapers are full of advertising. Some advertisements are tiny want ads. Others fill several pages. Sometimes what seems to be a comic strip may turn out to be advertising. Magazines, too, carry advertisements.

2. Fix the following sentences so that they say what you think the writer means, retaining as much as possible of the original wording. If you can't fix a sentence, state why.

a. Until the traffic was halted and the onlookers were herded to a safe distance.
b. The man dying shortly after noon sank into a peaceful coma late Friday morning.
c. The trolley lurched and crushing his nose threw the man to the floor.
d. The consultant first entered the building in April, hired to explore the concept of pay television.
e. Two separate resumes should be prepared and although each will contain some of the same information, they would be geared to different kinds of jobs and each is to present background information in a unique manner.
f. Another play is on the drawing board, which promises to benefit from having written the first.
g. The work load and responsibilities that millions of American women face and accomplish daily overwhelmed me.
h. The caravan of prairie schooners, filled with men who had come all the way from Spain, others had just joined them, headed west.
i. In a stern voice, Peder reminded the children do not fidget, sit up straight, and they weren't to take their eyes off him.
j. Outside he felt the cool late summer air carried a hint of autumn.
k. It was a sure bet that I would have my buck as soon as opening day would arrive.
l. As he opened the door, on the stove was cooking cereal.
m. Peter was thankful she said nothing but smiled when he poured the milk.
n. He still had the people he knew back home well in his mind.

o. She had not ridden in the car for several months, and today the trip reminded her of the first time when they saw the old farm.
p. I came to visit and we would talk about life.
q. What is often distressful is to discover one's thoughts and feelings particularly the worst ones like the rage and frustration I felt when at Christmas my plane connection was late which meant that I could not get to Minneapolis and then to Phoenix after I had made reservations six months in advance.
r. I have a friend who wears green and looks hideous and I have not said a word to her.
s. The unconscious, that's where.
t. The most usual problem people told me about was losing a person they cared for and were depressed.
u. Some people when separating can bounce back quite rapidly; others go into a blue funk; and if you're not bouncing back think about seeing someone who can help you through this difficult time.
v. Someone trained to listen, to help, who has been educated in psychotherapy.
w. Great when you have a physical disease, but not when you're feeling depressed.
x. He caught it as if it was a balloon.
y. Everybody should wash your hands for dinner.
z. She was a polite girl, or so it had always seemed to me.
aa. Clothes no longer can make the person in most places worth traveling.

6
CONJUNCTIONS AND PREPOSITIONS

A conjunction (sometimes called a *connective*) is a word or short group of words that joins. As we've seen in the previous chapter, it can join anything, from words to phrases to clauses to sentences. A preposition is a specific kind of conjunction. It joins an *object* noun or pronoun, along with all its various modifiers, to the rest of the sentence. By choosing one conjunction or preposition rather than another, you also show how what you're joining relates to the rest of the sentence. Most conjunctions are used so often in speaking, they give little trouble in writing. But there are a few that trip us all up. We'll concentrate on those, and the reasons for our difficulties.

Many of our modern-day conjunctions didn't exist as conjunctions until Modern English took hold in about the seventeenth century, although most of the words were already in the language being used for other parts of speech. The subordinating conjunctions *where, when, how,* and *why* had been adverbs. *Because* came from the phrase *by cause. After* developed from *of* and the comparative *-er* ending (which was *-ter* in Old English). *Provided* (in *provided that*) came from the past tense of the verb *provide. Due to,* one of the most recent additions, developed from the adjective *due*. *Of, to, for, by,* and *with* all show relationships that, in Old English, were shown by special word endings that have since been dropped from the language.

The trickiest thing about conjunctions is that grammar books say they can be two parts of speech in the same sentence. In the following sentence *where* is described as an adverb within its own clause (*where he spoke*), modifying the verb *spoke,* while within the sentence as a whole it is described as a coordinating conjunction.

> The platform where he spoke is now painted.

Here are two sentences which mean the same thing. But grammarians say that in the first sentence, *due* is an adjective and belongs with the verb *was,* while in the second sentence *due* is a preposition linked to the noun *coldness.*

> His refusal was due to the coldness of the weather.
> Due to the coldness of the weather, he refused.

Happily, outside grammar classes there's never a need to name a conjunction, just to use it properly.

CLUE 1: WHEN TO USE *THAT*

That is a conjunction that causes writers more headaches than all the rest combined. It is *always* needed to insert a clause right after *say* or *tell,* but *never* used right after *talk* or *speak*. It belongs after *ask* meaning *request*.

> He asked that I go.

But it never belongs after *ask* meaning *question.*

Jack asked whether John had solved the question.
Jack asked if John had solved the question.

That is often optional; we can put it in or leave it out.

He said that he would go.
He said he would go.

But sometimes omitting *that* clouds up the meaning or slows up the reading.

WRONG: He urged private industry team up with government in the fight against poverty.
CORRECT: He urged that private industry team up . . .

Sometimes leaving out *that* actually changes a sentence's meaning.

The bar features three windows with a view so relaxing skiers can view the summit.
The bar features three windows with a view so relaxing that skiers can view the summit.

To avoid confusion and misunderstanding, make it a habit to insert every *that* that's implied, even after the word *so*.

I'm taking the course so that I can get an A.

Catch 1: Don't Confuse *that* with *who*

In one use of *that* as a conjunction, it doubles as a relative pronoun. In the following sentence, *that* not only introduces the clause *that I am feeding,* but also—as a pronoun—refers back to *the dog*.

The dog that I am feeding is not hungry any more.

In spoken English, we sometimes use *that* in this combination pronoun/conjunction situation even when it refers to people.

COLLOQUIAL: The man that I met yesterday is late today.

But in standard written English, this usage is considered wrong. When you're referring to a particular person, always use *who* even when the pronoun is also a conjunction.

CORRECT: The man who(m) I met yesterday is late today.

(For further discussion of the *who/whom* controversy see page 21.)

On the other hand, when you're referring to a class or group of people whose names are unimportant, and not to particular people, old grammar books—and some old grammar teachers—instruct you to use *that,* not *who.*

She is the cheerleader who will lead the parade. (Of several specific cheerleaders)
It is a rare man that is never silent. (Of all men)

Subtle distinctions like this have made formal English formidable for students whose main concern—as it should be—is simply to be understood.

Catch 2: Don't Confuse *that* with *which*

The biggest battle raging today in grammatical circles is the battle over when to use *that* and when to use *which. That* is the oldest of the relative pronouns, going way back to Old English. In the fifteenth century, *which* came along, and at first it was simply an alternative.

SHAKESPEARE: Happy is your Grace, that can translate the stubbornness of fortune into so quiet and so sweet a style.

THE LORD'S PRAYER: Our Father, Which art in Heaven . . .

In the sixteenth century, *who* began to be used as a relative pronoun.

SHAKESPEARE: For treason is but trusted like the fox, who, ne'er so tame, so cherisht, and lockt up, will have a wild trick of his ancestors.

But it wasn't until the eighteenth century that people began to use *who* just for people and *which* just for animals and things.

As you may recall, the eighteenth century was when the early grammarians were so hard at work trying to make logic out of our language. They not only codified this difference between *who* and *which* (as well as the differences between *who* and *that* just described in Catch 1), they also came up with another distinction. They attempted to make us believe there's a time to use *which* and a time to use *that*. Their rule went:

> *That* should be used to introduce a defining or limiting clause.
>
> *Which* should be used only to introduce a nondefining or parenthetical clause (a clause that

can be put in parentheses or between commas or left out entirely without taking away from the full grammatical meaning of the rest of the sentence).

In the following sentence, because we use *that,* the clause that follows it defines the idea: it specifies which idea, out of several, I'm referring to.

> The idea that I had yesterday was a good one.

In the next sentence, the use of *which* makes the rest of the clause (*which I had yesterday*) into an aside, relegating it to relative unimportance.

> The idea which I had yesterday was a good one.

Though spoken English still uses *that* and *which* quite interchangeably, teachers who know the rule look for this grammatical usage. (Pedants who don't understand the rule have been known to change every *which* to *that* just to be on the safe side—which is comical since, fifty years ago, the same sort of pedants were changing every *that* to *which.*)

Here are a few guidelines to help you steer through the shoals of *who, which,* and *that.* (See also pages 24, 51, 65.)

1. Always use *who,* not *which* or *that,* to refer to people unless it's a general reference to an impersonal group.
2. In writing standard school English, always use *which* for parenthetical clauses and *that* for clauses that can't be put between parentheses.
3. Disregarding the above, whenever two *thats* come one after the other, for ease of reading (and no better reason) always change the second *that* to *which.*

> Nowhere could he find that which he'd been searching for.

To get around *that/whiches,* people often substitute *the one* for the first *that.*

> Nowhere could he find the one that he'd been searching for.

CLUE 2: SOME VERBS TAKE A SUBJUNCTIVE *THAT* CLAUSE

There are some verbs that, when followed by *that* (whether you write *that* or just imply it), always require the subjunctive form of the verb. (See page 51 to refresh your understanding of the subjunctive.) The most frequently used of those verbs are:

advise	insist	request
ask (when it means request)	prefer	require
demand	propose	suggest
forbid	recommend	urge

WRONG: He advised that she goes to a doctor.
CORRECT: He advised that she go to a doctor.

This form of the verb is so little used in modern English, people find it strange to say. Instead, alternate forms are favored both in speech and writing.

> He advised her to go to a doctor.
> He advised that she should go to a doctor.

If you're not sure of your subjunctives, it's a good idea to switch to one of these alternatives.

CLUE 3: FOUR TRICKY CONJUNCTION PAIRS

Once you can deal with *that, which,* and *who,* there are only four conjunction pairs to beware of. Learn their distinctions and you're home free.

like/as—A few years ago, an advertising slogan caught the ears and eyes of horrified grammarians everywhere. "Illiterate!" they cried. "Colloquial," responded the sloganeers. The slogan was:

> Winston tastes good like a cigarette should.

In speaking, we use *like* and *as* pretty interchangeably. And no wonder, since both words are derived from a much older idiom, *like as.* Nowadays, we even use *like* to mean *as if.* But the grammarians have taken *like* under their wing. They've ruled that you must never use *like* as a conjunction. If you're writing for sticklers, you'll be expected to follow that rule.

Sometimes the grammarians have a point. Read the following sentence.

> The old man swilled the brandy like he'd done it all his life.

It's conceivable for that sentence to have either of the following meanings.

> The old man swilled the brandy the way he'd done it all his life.
>
> The old man swilled the brandy as if he'd done it all his life.

When you do choose to use *like* for *as* or *as if* or *in the same way,* make certain that your sentence's meaning won't be misunderstood.

else/or else—The word *else,* used as a conjunction to mean *otherwise,* used to stand alone—and still does in some regions of the United States.

You'd better go else you'll get in trouble.

However, *else* has come to be so closely associated with other words (*somebody else, little else, all else, what else, who else*) that to many educated people it seems incorrect standing alone. That's why most people now insert *or.*

You'd better go or else you'll get in trouble.

Professors who aren't aware that *else* is correct sometimes mark it wrong unless *or* accompanies it. Forewarned is forearmed.

beside/besides—We discussed these two words in the *modifiers* chapter, but since they're also used as conjunctions they bear repeated mention.

Beside, in short, means *at the side of; besides* means *in addition to* or *furthermore.* Don't get caught writing *beside* when you mean *besides.*

I was beside myself, and besides, I was unhappy.

The conjunctive idiom is *besides that,* not *beside that.*

I was beside myself, and besides that, I was unhappy.

off/off of—Off is a conjunction; *off of* is not, though it's fighting hard for acceptance in our spoken language. It seems sensible, when we say *out of,* to also say *off of.* But as we've shown, language doesn't develop sensibly, and *off of* is still considered illiterate. If the extra word creeps in, erase it.

CLUE 4: WHEN TO END A SENTENCE WITH A PREPOSITION

Despite the adage, "Never end a sentence with a preposition," it's done all the time in spoken English—especially when that preposition is part of the previous verb. (See page 47.)

Pocahontas is the Indian the writer referred to.

Sometimes a preposition is put at the sentence's end for emphasis or rhythm.

Take home that novel and read it through.

But some old-timers still see sentence-ending prepositions as red flags. We once asked an old-timer, on a New York street, "Where's the subway at?" His answer: "Never end a sentence with a preposition." We corrected our error quickly: "Where's the subway at, pedant?" If you're writing for an old-timer, we suggest that you, too, bury your prepositions instead of waving them at sentence's end.

CHECKUP QUIZ

1. The following paragraphs* were written in colloquial English. Rewrite them in standard written English without destroying the flavor of the original.

During my early years back on the farm I distinctly remember how excited we kids would get when a salesman or cattle buyer would pull in the driveway to do some jawin'

* Reprinted with permission from "Buck Savvy" by Rev. Chuck Tews, *Wisconsin Sportsman,* vol. 10 no. 6, November–December 1981.

with my dad. We'd hang around the perimeter of the action with ears as big as all outdoors just straining to hear every word and chuckle that flowed from this 'important' visit. Most times there was nothing real important taking place but being young just seemed to include being nosy as all get-out.

A few years later I remember hanging around men who could draw me like a magnet every time the conversation would get around to deer hunting. I was all eyes and ears, often feeling like I was right behind that fallen tree when that big buck was jumped in '48 and fell at the report of one blast. Story after story would pour forth like a babbling stream with no end in sight. After each session I would feel like I really had a handle on this deer hunting thing and it would be a sure bet that I would have a buck hanging from a tree as soon as that brisk opening day would arrive.

Fortunately, I lived in Waupaca County and right in our back yard was a fair-sized piece of woods which offered excellent deer hunting. If I was patient long enough a buck would soon come ambling down the trail and after I'd empty my shotgun at him I would miraculously put him down for keeps. I thought that I really had this deer hunting thing by the hind legs.

Fifteen years later I knew better. The bucks didn't come as easy as they did in that little patch of woods behind the farmhouse where I had long ago discovered their favorite trails and hiding places. I soon found out that there was a whole lot of things that a deer hunter should know so that he can reasonably expect to score no matter where he or she chooses to hunt.

So, if I were a young hunter big on ears but short on experience I would find myself a group of hunters who would surely talk about the good old times but whose serious conversation would center in character around these four areas: stand location; rub and scrape hunting; lures and masking agents; and attitude. Over the years I have found that hunters who are successful almost every year are hunters who employ tactics which center around these four basic elements.

2. Revise the following passage* so that it is acceptable to the strictest grammarian.

Almost every hunter who uses a dog has, at some time or another, been stuck with a dog that refuses to hunt. Unfortunately, by the time most people recognize the dog is worthless, substantial time and money have already been invested in the animal and even worse, the kids are in love with it, making putting it down out of the question.

Careful inquiry about the origin of these dogs, in about 99 cases out of 100, shows they came from one of three places—a "puppy mill", a backyard breeder, or from bench stock. Fortunately, there are ways to avoid making this costly mistake. You don't have to be a dog expert either. There are a few simple guidelines to remember when you select a pup which, in most cases will save you the trauma of getting a dog from one of these three sources.

A reputable breeder will tell you immediately if his dogs come from bench stock. But, if the breeder does not volunteer information on the background of his dogs or does not ask you how you intend to use the pup, it's time to be at least mildly suspicious. You may be walking into an expensive trap.

Ruth Elizabeth Foster, president of the Purebred Dog Breeders Association and a breeder of golden retrievers says, "Puppy mills are responsible for turning more people away from hunting with a dog than any other single cause. These people generally demonstrate a casual disregard for record keeping, among other problems. Frequently registration papers have no relationship to a particular animal except for breed, sex, and color. As many as 20 or more females may be in the same pen with two or more males, all of which are unidentified. As a result, pups are usually sold with either forged papers or papers belonging to some other dog."

---

* Excerpted with permission from "Beware of the Puppy Mills!" by M. J. Nelson, *Wisconsin Sportsman,* vol. 10 no. 6, November–December 1981.

Another trick used by puppy mill operators is to state a litter contains several more pups than it actually does. For example, if a litter contained six pups, they would send a litter registration application saying it contained 10. Then, they would have four extra registration applications to use where mismating with either unregistered dogs or dogs of another breed occur.

The shenanigans with registration papers may be these operations' most serious crime.

7
PUNCTUATION*

In speaking the English language, we use voice levels (loud and soft, as well as high and low pitch) and pauses to help show what our words mean. Punctuation in writing does the same job as those voice levels and pauses. If you say your sentences in your head when you write, you should get your punctuation correct nearly all the time. For guidance—or reassurance—here is a list of the major punctuation marks and how they compare to spoken equivalents. Although the period and question mark are rarely misused, let's begin with them for comparison.

CLUE 1: PUNCTUATING BY EAR

Period: The voice pitch and volume fall, then stop on a conclusive note to signal that a complete thought or series of related ideas has ended.

Question mark: The voice pitch and volume rise, then stop as long as for a period.

---

* Excerpted from *Good Writing* by Kesselman-Turkel and Peterson (Franklin Watts, 1981).

Comma: The voice pauses without its pitch or volume falling noticeably, to signal that one idea segment within a sentence has ended and another one is beginning. If your meaning is unquestionably clear without a pause—or comma—then the comma probably is not required.

> At any rate (,) almost immediately (,) the bottom fell out of both her world and his.

Colon: The voice stops abruptly, but with emphasis that shows that an elaboration of the just-completed idea will continue immediately.

> In most cases, the co-worker is not malignant in intent but just someone who wants something you have and really doesn't give a damn how you feel: a conflict where most learners have no difficulty in refusing to give reasons to justify or explain their behavior to the other person.

Dashes: The voice pauses at the first dash, emphasizes slightly the material set between dashes, and resumes its former tone after the second dash, showing that another thought is interrupting the sentence's normal flow of thoughts. When the emphasized material ends the sentence, only the first dash is needed; a period ends both the emphasized portion and the entire sentence. As with all other forms of emphasis, when it's overused the dash loses its impact.

Years ago dashes were little used, and parentheses preferred to commas. (That's why asides put between commas are still referred to in many grammars as parenthetical phrases.) Our modern system is a refinement in reader signals. Set between dashes, the interrupting idea is flagged by the author as important. Set between commas, it is shown to be neither more nor less important than its neighbors. Parentheses are for relatively unimportant asides.

Another mistake novices make is to use the dash where a

colon is the better choice. Keep in mind that the dash signals an emphasized aside, whereas a colon signals a to-the-point elaboration.

> I sat on the metal cot—there was no chair—and stared around my cell.

Some writers use a great many dashes in their writing. This usually signals to the reader either that the writer has not organized his thoughts into logical units, or that he has not taken the time to decide what should or should not be emphasized. If lots of dashes creep into your writing, it's a signal to stop and decide whether all the asides are really important and, if so, whether they ought to be elaborated on separately.

Parentheses: The voice pauses, then de-emphasizes the information set between parentheses. This punctuation device is supposed to clarify a thought without shifting the reader's attention to the clarification. It isn't as effective as most of our punctuation marks because it slows down the eye, often creating the emphasis it's trying to avoid. That's why it's a good idea to resist parentheses unless they're indispensable.

Underline: The voice emphasizes the word or words underlined. Careful writers pick words and sentence constructions that emphasize naturally, and use underlining only as a last resort. Careless writers make it a crutch, attempting with it to impart drama to a particular point that otherwise falls flat.

The underline rarely appears in print; when a typesetter sees it, he substitutes italics.

Exclamation point: The exclamation point is an attempt to instill drama into an entire sentence. But if the sentence itself isn't dramatic, no amount of flashing marquee lights at the end will convince the reader otherwise. In English (unlike Spanish) the exclamation point appears only at the end of the sentence, not at the beginning. Save exclamation points for true exclamations—the short bursts of sentence fragment that share strong feelings with readers.

> "Peace!" he cried. "Only peace!"

Quotation marks: Voice inflections, pauses, and mimicry signal that you're speaking somebody else's words. On paper they are conveyed with quotation marks.

Sometimes quotation marks are used by writers to disown words: to show the reader that the writer knows they're slang, or are used unconventionally, or express ideas with which the writer doesn't agree. Readers faced with this use of quotes seldom know why the word or phrase is being disowned, and the device generally ends up looking sophomoric.

> The eternal stillness outside my door formed a barrier protecting my soul. I could "hear myself think."

If the reason for your disavowal is important, take the time to discuss it. If not, don't make an issue of your small difference of opinion.

CLUE 2: OTHER PUNCTUATION MARKS

Several forms of punctuation used in writing don't have counterparts in oral communication. The following three add sophistication to the expression of ideas, and are therefore worth including in the writer's arsenal. Keep in mind that punctuation is a convenience to the reader, not the writer (who usually knows already how his sentences should read).

Semicolon: The semicolon is usually used as a weakened period. It joins two sentences, each of which is grammatically complete. But it signals that the ideas are so closely related that, for maximum clarity, the two sentences ought to be read as one.

> I have experimented with some mitecides, in desperation over a particular mango tree I simply could not bear to dispose of; however, I have found them ineffective in the long run.

On occasion, writers use the semicolon as a supercomma. In a string of thoughts, commas ordinarily separate the individual thoughts. But if one or more of the thoughts itself has to contain a comma for clear meaning, the reader may become confused about what's coordinate and what's subordinate. In such cases, most writers employ semicolons to signal the wider separations.

> They most frequently strike in three areas: where ocean plates are thrusting under land plates, as is happening along the coasts of Alaska and Central Indonesia and the Caribbean; where the plates are grinding past each other, as in California and Turkey; and where continents are running into each other, as in China, Iran, and the countries of the Balkans and eastern Mediterranean, which are slowly crumpling under the pressure exerted by northward-moving India, Arabia and Africa, respectively.

Ellipsis: a series of three dots signals to readers that you've left out some words. At the end of a sentence, where a period is required, a fourth dot should be added.

> "This investigation . . . on its surface has an overwhelming appearance of a simple, wide-ranging exposure campaign . . . ," stated Supreme Court Justice Brennan.

Brackets: When you want to quote another author's exact words, but don't want to be bound by just those words, brackets provide an effective escape. If, for instance, all you need to quote is one sentence, but the sentence is unclear out of context, you can provide the missing information within brackets.

> "It [his bungalow] was on a side street."

In informal writing, authors often omit the word which requires explanation.

> "[His bungalow] was on a side street, smothered . . ."

Avoid brackets wherever possible. Here's an alternative.

> His bungalow "was on a side street, smothered . . ."

Brackets are also used to insert corrections and author's asides within quoted matter. The word *sic,* which tells the reader that the author is reproducing an error that was in the original quotation, also goes within brackets or within parentheses. Brackets should be used for parenthetical information that's set within an already parenthesized statement.

> Use brackets (or parentheses [see previous section]) around the word *sic.*

CHECKUP QUIZ

1. Punctuate the following paragraph.

Despite the original definition of the word sweepstakes winner take all the format that's evolved over the years is a pyramid of prizes. At the top you got to put a big flashy grand prize says Don Jagoda sweepstakes consultant for Cracker Jack. He adds the most popular top prize is money a big chunk of cold cash the trouble with cash of course is that you can't buy money wholesale the second-best choice is a car or a trip.

2. Correct the punctuation in the following sentences.

a. Boots, snowshoes, and even “woolies” come in handy when you're in the woods in late fall.
b. Take your long johns or you'll regret it!
c. “Too cold” my bones protest and the shadows say “too dark go back to bed”.
d. Did you ever ask a man to lend his pet fly rod—or his oldest carpet slippers?
e. As soon as the nostrils of the big doe got a whiff of the scent she immediately stopped and later moved on by picking her way through the woods.
f. The administrators who staffed the committee made their preliminary report in December, 1981 and in it identified several options.
g. The committee will meet on March 24—place to be announced later—to seek public reaction to their plan.
h. A sauna is a simple (easy-to-make) structure that is also inexpensive to build.
i. Vitamin A is a “raw material” responsible for growth and repair of tissues, particularly those of the eyes skin hair teeth and bones.
j. Recent information confirms: Vitamin A helps regulate and stabilize blood sugar.
k. Those of us on hectic work schedules miss more than an occasional “sensible” meal.
l. The Recommended Dietary Allowance—RDA—for these vitamins is a matter of record.
m. At first the sky was grey, later the sun came out.

ANSWERS TO CHECKUP QUIZZES

Score as shown. If you score less than 90% on any quiz, review that section. If you score less than 65%, buy and use a large grammar handbook.

NOUNS (100 IS PERFECT SCORE)

1. Score ½ point for each correct answer (total: 42 points).

	noun?	*sing. poss.*	*pl. poss.*
roar	S	roar's (rare)	roars' (rare)
ligament	A	ligament's	ligaments'
life raft	A	life raft's	life rafts'
size	S	size's	sizes'
equally	N		
droopy	N		
lift-off	A	lift-off's	lift-offs'
equation	A	equation's	equations'
brass	S	brass's	brasses'
Jones	A	Jones's	Joneses'
lady	A	lady's	ladies'
who	N		

	noun?	*sing. poss.*	*pl. poss.*
craze	S	craze's	crazes'
to	N		
lens	A	lens's	lenses'
to dream	S	(none)	
so	N		
equate	N		
Staten Island	A	Staten Island's	(none)
very	N		
dinnerware	A	dinnerware's	(none)
pity	S	pity's	(none)
blessing	S	blessing's (rare)	blessings' (rare)
to blossom	S	(none)	
communism	A	communism's	(none)
dancing	S	dancing's (rare)	(none)
elf	A	elf's	elves'
ghetto	A	ghetto's	ghettos' or ghettoes'
anybody else	N*	anybody else's	(none)

* This idiom is, strictly speaking, a pronoun, not a noun.

2. Score 3 points for each correct answer.

piano player (*not* player piano)
nailbrush
nail file
birdseed
goosedown
moonbeam
comet tail
guest towel
war victims
community citizens
communist philosophy*

* The shift here occurs mainly because it's hard to speak the phrase *communism philosophy*. Many words that seem exceptions to rules are the result of an attempt to make speech simpler or more comfortable.

3. Score 1 point for each correct answer. They are, in order:

Don Roux
business
sweepstakes
people
telling
sweepstakes'
appeal
professors
marketing
seminar
Wayne State University
games of chance
professors
hands
hour's
lecture
Roux
business card
bottom
chair
stereo
person
skeptics
chairs

PRONOUNS (98 IS PERFECT SCORE)

1. Score 2 points for each correct answer.

a. who, his
b. he, himself
c. nobody, it

d. me, those
e. each, these, its
f. one, one's (equally acceptable: she, her)
g. one, oneself or one's self (less formal: one, himself or herself)
h. everybody, he or she (if you said *they're* score 1 pt.), someone
i. themselves
j. his or her (*not* their)
k. its (This means that the choir is writing as a group. If each member is writing a song, the sentence should read: The choir [members] are writing their own songs. For clarity, we would insert the word *members*.)
l. their, they, them (not *it* since the pronoun refers to the plural noun *methods*)

2. Score 2 points for each correct answer.

a. its
b. yours, his, theirs
c. whose
d. himself
e. there's, whose
f. I, whom
g. whoever
h. whom
i. one
j. one's, are
k. stops
l. does
m. does, his
n. theirs
o. it's, I, am
p. theirs
q. I, am (the verb reflects the person of the final pronoun of a series), us

VERBS (98 IS PERFECT SCORE)

1. Score 2 points for each correct answer.

After class I laid my books on the table and set myself down (score 1 point for sat down) on a chair that I dragged alongside (score 4 points extra if you deleted up) it. All at once I saw a paper lying there that I could have sworn I had given to my sister the day before. She probably had hoped to hide it from me, because it looked like it was torn. I would have preferred (rather cannot be used as a verb in written English) she'd told (had told is okay too) me. Next time I lend something to her, she would do better not to rip it up and then try to squirrel it out of sight. I would not have lent it to her in the first place if I had known (I'd have known is okay) that she had become unable (she'd become unable is okay; score 1 point for she'd gotten unable) to take care of things.

2. Score 2 points for each correct answer.

a. will
b. won't
c. became or was; score 1 point for *got,* but do not use it in formal writing or speech.
d. into (if you choose *up to,* you run the danger of being misread because of the idiom *beat up*)
e. up
f. to
g. were (the idiom *a number* means several)
h. gave, are
i. gets (if this were a command, there'd be a comma after *everybody*)
j. is
k. were
l. up (*come on* means something else)

3. Score 2 points for every correct answer.

's	stuck up
promoting	announced
knows	had taped
can be	would send
delights	found
demonstrated	should have seen
asked	turning over
were . . . motivated	says

MODIFIERS (103 IS PERFECT SCORE)

1. Score 3 points for each correct answer. Subtract 3 points for each word circled incorrectly.

most—adv.
talented—adj.
down—adv. (score 3 points if you considered it part of the verb *track down*)
ferocious—adj.
such—adv.
great—adj.
totally—adv.
spongy—adj.
behind—adv.
tangled—adj.
steamy—adj.
(sheep ranches is a compound noun. Subtract 1 point if you circled sheep or ranches.)
medical—adj.
(detective story is a compound noun)
certainly—adv.
most—adv.

lovely—adj.
best—adj. (modifies *thrillers*)
science-fiction—adj.

2. Score 2 points for each correct answer. (Corrections are underlined.) Subtract 2 points for each incorrect change.

a. The awful question is whether television will continue to satisfy these sorts of people. (or this sort of person)
b. Don't miss out on this opportunity since it's your last chance.
c. When I got this boat, it sure reminded them of those sails hidden away over there. (Score ½ point if you changed sure to surely.)
d. He just sat there staring blankly at the screen, wanting badly to get up and go somewhere else.
e. It sure is mighty kind of you to sweat so mightily in my behalf. (Be sure to subtract 2 points for each change you incorrectly made.)
f. He kept an awfully chilly silence under the still, lonely moon, though they sure tried hard and mightily to make him yell out. (Score 2 points for: He kept an awful, chilly. . . .)
g. This sure has been the coldest day of the year. (delete most)
h. I'm sure going to be more nearly perfect the next time I try this crummy exercise.

i. Broadcasting is the most persuasive means of communication ever known, and even more entertaining than persuasive. (Alternate: Broadcasting is the most persuasive means of communication ever known and, even more, it's entertaining.)
j. This ring is even more nearly unique than that one.
k. He's a likely candidate for the job, but she's the most likely to get it. (or she's the likeliest . . .)

l. Nobody wants it more badly than he. (Score 2 points for each word.)
m. Hardly had he picked up the lonely pup than the phone rang.
n. This might explain why it can lie dormant for a few months, and then spring to life instantaneously.
o. If she hadn't looked so sweet and sunny, then I wouldn't have behaved so evilly.
p. This trip wasn't any different from the last, except that the natives spoke differently and the guide wore different clothes.
q. In this case, I'm not any worse off than he. (Score 1 point for him.)

SENTENCES (100 IS PERFECT SCORE)

1. You'll have to score yourself subjectively here, because there are many right answers to this question. Here's ours. (Score from 0 to 9 points for part a, and from 0 to 10 points for part b.)

a. Bob and Ben fell from the little sled, getting wet, but the sled did not stop. It ran on and on, into a red barn. The barn bent the little sled, and the sled dented the barn.

   (Subtract 6 points from your score if you didn't move the idea in the last sentence up to where it belongs.)
b. Every day we see and hear a great deal of advertising: the words and pictures on our box of breakfast cereal and our carton of milk, the commercial on radio or television, the contents of most of the circulars our letter carrier brings. Newspapers and magazines are packed full of tiny want ads up to multi-page spreads. Sometimes what seems to be a comic strip turns out to be advertising.

(Deduct 3 points for each time you repeated *see* or *hear,* and for every time—beyond the first 3—you used *ad* or *advertisement.*

2. Score 3 points for each correct sentence. Here again, in some cases your answer may vary slightly from ours.

a. This is a sentence fragment containing just a subordinate clause; the independent clause, containing the subject of the sentence, is missing.
b. The man sank into a peaceful coma late Friday morning, dying shortly after noon.
c. The trolley lurched and threw the man to the floor, crushing his nose.
d. The consultant first entered the building in April, having been hired to explore the concept of pay television.
e. Two separate resumes should be prepared and, although both (or: *each*) should contain some of the same information, each should present background information in a unique manner since they will be geared to different kinds of jobs. (Subtract 2 points if you kept your *each* clauses separated.)
f. Another play is on the drawing board and (or: *that*) promises to benefit from his having written the first.
g. I was overwhelmed by the work load and responsibilities daily faced and accomplished by millions of American women.
h. The caravan of prairie schooners headed west, filled with men who had come all the way from Spain and others who had just joined them.
i. In a stern voice, Peder reminded the children not to fidget, to sit up straight, and not to take their eyes off him.
j. Outside he felt the cool late summer air that carried a hint of autumn. (Or: Outside, he felt, the cool late summer air carried a hint of autumn.)

k. It was a sure bet that I would have my buck as soon as opening day arrived.
l. As he opened the door, cereal was cooking on the stove.
m. Peter was thankful that she said nothing but he smiled when he poured the milk. (Alternate: Peter was thankful that, though she said nothing, she smiled when he poured the milk.)
n. He still had well in his mind the people he knew back home. (Or: He still had in his mind the people he knew well back home.)
o. She had not ridden in the car for several months, and today the trip reminded her of the first time that they'd seen the old farm. (Or: She had not ridden in the car for several months, and today the trip reminded her of the first time, when they'd seen the old farm.)
p. I came to visit and we talked about life. (Or: I would come to visit and we would talk about life.)
q. It is often distressful to discover one's thoughts and feelings, particularly the worst ones. My worst were the rage and frustration I felt when, at Christmas, my plane connection was late after I had made reservations six months in advance, and I could not get to Minneapolis and then to Phoenix. (Subtract 2 points if you did not create two separate sentences or change *one's* to *my*.)
r. I have a friend who wears green hideously (or: and looks hideous in it) and I have not said a word to her about it. (Or: I have a friend who looks hideous in green and I have not said a word to her about it.)
s. This is a sentence fragment. The verb is missing.
t. The most usual problem people told me about was losing a person they cared for and being depressed.
u. Some people, when separating, can bounce back quite rapidly; others go into a blue funk. If you're not bouncing back, think about seeing someone who can help you through this difficult time.
v. This is a sentence fragment. There is no verb, just a subject and its modifiers.

w. This fragment has no subject and no verb, just an adverb (*great*) and two subordinate clauses.

x. He caught it as if it were a balloon.

y. Everybody should wash his or her (alternate: their) hands for dinner. (Or: You should wash your hands for dinner.)

z. She was a polite girl, or so she had always seemed to me. (This is an example of absence of agreement.)

aa. In most places worth traveling, clothes no longer make the person. (The sentence in error was actually copied that way from a newspaper article. It points out how silly a sentence can sound if you don't put your ideas in the correct order.)

CONJUNCTIONS AND PREPOSITIONS (100 IS PERFECT SCORE)

There are many right answers to each part of this quiz, which requires a knowledge of all the information covered in the book. Using our changes as a guide, score yourself from 0 to 50 points for each passage. Better, ask to be scored by a friend whose grammar is excellent.

1. Be sure to subtract 1 point for each wrong verb form you didn't correct.

During my early years back on the farm, I distinctly remember, how excited we kids would get when a salesman or cattle buyer pulled in the driveway to do some jawing with my dad. We'd hang around the perimeter of the action with ears as big as all outdoors, straining to hear every word and chuckle that flowed from this important visit. Most times there was nothing really important taking place, but being young seemed to include being nosy as all get-out.

A few years later, I remember, I hung around men who

could draw me like a magnet every time the conversation got around to deer hunting. I was all eyes and ears, often feeling as if I were right behind that fallen tree where the big buck had been jumped in '48 and had fallen at the report of one blast. Story after story would pour forth like a babbling stream with no end in sight. After each session, I would feel as if I really had a handle on deer hunting, and as if it were a sure bet that I would have a buck hanging from a tree as soon as that brisk opening day arrived.

Fortunately, I lived in Waupaca County and right in our back yard was a fair-sized piece of woods that offered excellent deer hunting. If I were to be patient long enough, a buck must (or: *was sure to,* or: *had to*) soon come ambling down the trail and, when I emptied my shotgun at him, I must (or: *was sure to,* or: *had to*) miraculously put him down for keeps. I thought that I really had deer-hunting by the hind legs.

Fifteen years later I knew better. The bucks didn't come as easily as they did in that little patch of woods behind the farmhouse where I had long ago discovered their favorite trails and hiding places. I soon found out that there were a whole lot of things that a deer hunter should know before he or she can reasonably expect to score no matter where he or she chooses to hunt.

So if I were a young hunter big on ears but short on experience, I would find myself a group of hunters who surely would talk about the good old times, but whose serious conversation would center on these four subjects: stand location, rub and scrape hunting, lures and masking agents, and attitude. Over the years I have found that hunters who employ these four basic tactics are successful almost every year.

2. Subtract 5 points if you haven't condensed paragraph 2, and 5 points if you haven't corrected the garbled quotation.

Almost every hunter who uses a dog has at some time or other been saddled with a dog that refuses to hunt. Unfortunately, in the case of most people, by the time it's recognized that the dog is worthless, substantial time and money have already been invested in the animal. Even worse, the children are in love with it, and disposing of the dog becomes out of the question.

Careful inquiry into the origin of dogs who refuse to hunt, shows that in about 99 cases out of 100, they come from one of three places: a puppy mill, a backyard breeder, or bench stock. Fortunately, you don't have to be a dog expert to avoid, in most cases, the trauma of finding yourself with a dog from one of these three sources. There are a few simple guidelines to remember when you're selecting a pup.

A reputable breeder will tell you immediately if his dogs come from bench stock. If the breeder does not volunteer information on his dog's background or ask how you intend to use the puppy, be suspicious. You may be walking into an expensive trap.

Ruth Elizabeth Foster, president of the Purebred Dog Breeders' Association and a breeder of golden retrievers, says, "Puppy mills are more responsible for dissuading people from hunting with dogs than any other single cause. Puppy mill owners generally demonstrate a casual disregard for recordkeeping. Frequently, a particular animal's registration papers correctly show only its breed, sex, and color. As many as 20 (or: *more than 20*) females may be in the same pen with two or more males, all of the dogs unidentified. As a result, puppies are usually sold with either forged papers or papers belonging to some other dog."

Another trick used by puppy mill operators is to register a litter containing several more puppies than it actually does. For example, if a litter contains six puppies, an operator may send a litter registration application saying that it contains ten. Then the operator has four extra registration applications to use when mismating occurs with either unregistered dogs or dogs of another breed.

Shenanigans with registration papers may be the most serious crime of these puppy mill operators.

PUNCTUATION (99 IS PERFECT SCORE)

1. Score 1½ points for each correct punctuation mark inserted, and subtract 1½ points for each incorrect one.

Despite the original definition of the word sweepstakes, winner take all, *(dashes are also correct)* the format that's evolved over the years is a pyramid of prizes. "At the top you got to put a big, flashy grand prize," says Don Jagoda, sweepstakes consultant for Cracker Jack. He adds, "The most popular top prize is money, a big chunk of cold cash; the trouble with cash, of course, is that you can't buy money wholesale. The second-best choice is a car or a trip."

2. Score 6 points for each correct sentence.

a. Boots, snowshoes, and even woolies come in handy when you're in the woods in late fall.
b. Take your long johns or you'll regret it.
c. "Too cold," my bones protest, and the shadows say, "Too dark. Go back to bed."
d. Did you ever ask a man to lend his pet fly rod or his oldest carpet slippers?
e. As soon as the nostrils of the big doe got a whiff of the scent, she immediately stopped, and later moved on by, picking her way through the woods. (Moved on by, . . . and moved on by . . . are both okay.)
f. The administrators who staffed the committee made their preliminary report in December, 1981, and in it identified several options.
g. The committee will meet on March 24 (place to be announced later) to seek public reaction to their plan.
h. A sauna is a simple, easy-to-make structure that is also inexpensive to build.

i. Vitamin A is a raw material responsible for growth and repair of tissues, particularly those of the eyes, skin, hair, teeth, and bones.

j. Recent information confirms that Vitamin A helps regulate and stabilize blood sugar.

k. Those of us on hectic work schedules miss more than an occasional sensible meal.

l. The Recommended Dietary Allowance (RDA) for these vitamins is a matter of record.

m. At first the sky was grey; later the sun came out.

INDEX